Look into the stillness
A spiritual journey through inspirational quotes

By

Donald L. Hicks

© Copyright 2015, Donald L. Hicks

All rights reserved.
No part of this book, in part or in whole, may be reproduced, stored in a retrieval system, or
transmitted by any means, electronic, mechanical, photocopying, recording, or
otherwise, without written permission from the author, except for brief quotations embodied in literary
articles and reviews.

Material in this book is for educational purposes or spiritual consideration only. This book is sold with
the understanding that neither the author nor the publisher is engaged in rendering legal, accounting,
investment, medical, or any other professional service.

For permission, or serialization, condensation, adaptions, write to: Nature's Path, 5721 Flinn Lane,
Amelia Court House, VA 23002

Library of Congress Cataloging-in-Publication Data
Hicks, Donald L. – 1962
"Look into the stillness" by Donald L. Hicks
Library of Congress Catalog Card Number: 2015935285

"A spiritual journey through inspirational quotes"

Printed in Charleston, South Carolina, USA

ISBN 13: 978-0692398210 (Nature's Path)
ISBN 10: 069239821X

Nature's Path
5721 Flinn Lane,
Amelia Court House, Virginia, USA
23002

Contents

Dedication: 6
What others are saying: 7
Prologue 9
Part 1: Love 13
Chapter 1 – Love yourself 15
Chapter 2 – Love Life 17
Chapter 3 -- Unconditional Love 19
Chapter 4 -- Love observing Love 23
Chapter 5 – The Language of Love 25
Part 2: Fear 30
Chapter 6 – Fear is darkness 32
Chapter 7 – Fear as a tool 37
Chapter 8 – Fear's reflection 39
Chapter 9 – Light overcomes darkness 42
Part 3: Perception 46
Chapter 10 – Looking for goodness 48
Chapter 11 – The beauty of color 50
Chapter 12 – Imperfect perfections 53
Chapter 13—Curves in the path 56
Chapter 14 – Creating good days 59
Chapter 15 – The power of thought 61
Chapter 16 – Soaring with imagination 64
Part 4: Life 68
Chapter 17 – The party of life 70
Chapter 18 – Life nurtures 72
Chapter 19 – Be a master 74
Chapter 20 – To Be or not to Be 78
Chapter 21 – Be the light 82
Chapter 22 – A lesson from plants 85
Chapter 23 – A gift for you 89
Chapter 24 – Releasing Fear 93
Chapter 25 – Freeing others 97
Chapter 26 – Lest ye be judged 99
Chapter 27 – Be surrounded with light 103
Chapter 28 – The presence of Truth 105

- Chapter 29 – Guided by the light ... 109
- Chapter 30 – Sacred life ... 112
- Part 5: Nature ... 118
- Chapter 31 – Nature, the teacher ... 120
- Chapter 32 – Nature, the giver ... 122
- Chapter 33 – Nature, the provider ... 124
- Chapter 34 – Nature, the artist ... 126
- Chapter 35 – Nature, as God expressed ... 129
- Chapter 36 – Nature, as God's chapel ... 133
- Chapter 37 – Nature's priests ... 137
- Chapter 38 – Nature's masters ... 141
- Chapter 39 – Nature, Life, and God ... 145
- Part 6: Finding God ... 150
- Chapter 40 – Losing your mind, finding God ... 152
- Chapter 41 – You are worthy ... 160
- Chapter 42 – Loving inspiration ... 165
- Chapter 43 – Practicing intuition ... 167
- Chapter 44 – Look into the Stillness ... 176
- Chapter 45 – Speaking for God ... 178
- Part 7: An encore of miscellaneous "Pearls of Wisdom" ... 182
- Contentment ... 184
- Oneness ... 185
- Faith ... 186
- God, Life and Love ... 187
- Separateness ... 188
- The Cold Shoulder ... 189
- Eternal Relationships ... 190
- Peace ... 191
- About the Author ... 192

God is not jealous.

God is not angry.

God is not vengeful.

You're thinking of someone else.

You're thinking of Fear.

Love never envies.

Love is always Joyful.

Love always forgives.

See the difference?

Now you know God.

Now you know Love.

Now you know there is no distinction between God and Love.

Dedication:

This book is dedicated to:

God and Nature, for all the inspiration they bring me.

To my wife, for handling many of my duties so I could write those inspirations.

To supportive friends, who encouraged me while my wife was handling my chores.

To James Wawro, for connecting me with a wonderful publisher and offering some sound and sage advice throughout the process. To everyone who has helped with this project, please know that I am grateful, and always remember:

"Every act of kindness is another step up Heaven's stairway."

You are now each many steps closer, and

you are loved.

What others are saying:

Look into the Stillness is one of those magical books where the simply written text quietly eases the reader into daydreams of how the book's themes actually play out in the reader's own life. In this way, the reader co-creates the story with author Donald L. Hicks and makes the stories in *Look into the Stillness* the reader's own—a masterful exercise in the art of storytelling.

-- James Wawro, author of ***Ask Your Inner Voice*** and ***Awakening Counsel***

In ***Look into the Stillness***, Donald L. Hicks shares the wisdom he has gleaned from his personal life experiences and his meditative connection with Nature. This book will inspire us to contemplate the essence of the Love-Fear dichotomy that we all face on a day-to-day basis, as well as the divine affinity of Love, Nature, and God. The author's sagacious guidance about embracing Love for ourselves, all other humans, and all flora and fauna found in Nature, blazes a trail leading to greater happiness and fulfillment in our lives through a more intimate communion with God.

--Garnet Schulhauser, author of ***Dancing on a Stamp*** and ***Dancing Forever with Spirit***

Prologue

I'd like to open this book by saying, it is no coincidence this book fell into your hands. Whether you believe that God led you to it, or a guardian angel, or your higher self, or simply while thumbing through the pages one of the quotes caught your eye, there is a reason you are now reading this book. I do not know that reason. You may not yet know the reason. But through the beauty of synchronicity that visits each of our lives, the reason(s) will soon be revealed.

As you read these pages, you may find that my beliefs about God and Life are different from your own beliefs. Please know that I do not consider my path a "better" path than anyone else's. Mine is simply a different path I'd like to share with those who would listen. For emphasis, I'd like to re-iterate that:

My path is not a better path, it is simply a different path.

To me, *how* a person most comfortably connects with God holds little importance. What's important is that people take brief respites from Life and connect. Whether it's yoga, or meditation, or prayer, or simply being still and listening to the tiny whispering voice inside, a successful connection is more important than the method. I would say, however, that if you begin a practice of meditation, strange-yet-wonderful things will begin to occur in your life.

Over the years, through my own connection (I like to sit quietly amid Nature), numerous "quotable" sayings have just "popped into my mind". Without sounding pretentious, I like to call them "pearls of wisdom", knowing they come from a Higher Source than just my mind and ego. A few of them contained such breathtaking wisdom and insight that I briefly entertained the idea I was a genius. I quickly concluded, however, that it's much more likely my mind is an empty and barren wasteland, which makes it easier for God, or my Higher Self, to sow these seeds for thought.

During these same years, I also learned that if I didn't immediately write down at least a fragment of these "pearls of wisdom", I would often forget them. I can't recall how many times I've been driving down the road, or peacefully meditating beneath a sprawling oak tree, and a thought would come to me, only to be forgotten by the time I reached a pen and paper.

Fortunately, I managed to record nearly 50 pages worth of short quotes, and as we make our journey here, we'll cover a portion of these, especially the ones that apply to the topics of Life, Love, Fear, Nature, Perception, Forgiveness, and God. My hope is that, through sharing them, they will bless and enrich your life as much as they have my own.

Part 1: Love

Chapter 1 – Love yourself

My three simple rules; it's as easy as 1,2,3:

#1. Love yourself and keep yourself from harm.
#2. Try to love everyone and everything you encounter.
#3. If someone or something from #2 causes you harm, refer to rule #1.

Rule #1: *Love yourself and keep yourself from harm.*

What's important to understand is, before you can correctly love anyone, you must first love yourself, and keep yourself from harm.

Many of us grew up learning the importance of loving others and treating others as we wish to be treated. But if you think about it, what good is "Loving thy neighbor *as thyself*" if you don't love thyself?

It's paramount that we love ourselves before we love others. Because, how can we honestly believe that others could love us if we don't find ourselves love-worthy?

For many people, not loving themselves can become a self-fulfilling prophecy. If they don't believe they are worthy of love, it's hard to believe that anyone else could love them for Who They Are. So when someone else proclaims they love that person, they doubt the authenticity of the claim, and often worry that the "lover" doesn't really love them for Who They Are, but simply because of *what they do for the lover*. This often leads the person into subconsciously sabotaging the relationship to see if the lover will "pine" for them, or using subtle "tests" to check the validity of the love. And if the "lover" fails any of these tests … even inadvertently or accidentally … the person ends the relationship. Ending the relationship then causes them to feel even worse about themselves, and less worthy of love.

The second part of the problem is, many of us feel guilty loving ourselves because we believe it will make us selfish. But the truth is, loving yourself doesn't make you selfish. When done correctly, *the exact opposite occurs*, because you know that selfish behaviors are negative for your mind, body and spirit.

Let me provide an example: if you give yourself permission to love yourself, are you going to suddenly rush to your freezer and scarf down the remainder of a gallon of ice cream just because you now love yourself, and you didn't before?

Of course not.

Because you … your mind, body, and spirit… are loved by You, and you understand that being a glutton is bad for you.

Will you suddenly begin indulging in all types of bad behavior?

Again, of course not… because loving yourself makes you less likely to indulge in bad behaviors. If anything, loving yourself will make you more likely to exercise, or meditate, and take care of the mind, body, and spirit that you love.

"You yourself, as much as anybody in the entire universe, deserve your love and affection." -- attributed to Gautama Siddharta, the Buddha[ii]

So please, give yourself permission to love yourself.

If others can find reasons to love you, you can find reasons to love you. So again, please, fall in love with you. Go ahead. It's okay. Be in love, and be Love.

Chapter 2 – Love Life

iii

Make your life a magical journey of Life, encountering Life.

Rule #2: *Try to love everyone and everything you encounter.*

It goes without saying that life can be difficult. Life can be staggering, or stunning. Life can dazzle us, or leave us feeling dazed. Life can be breathtaking, or it can knock the wind from our sails. Life is glorious, yet at times gloomy. It is fascinating, yet frightening. Life can be all of these things, because life is what we make it.

Life is not something that happens *to* us, Life happens *through* us.

Our challenge is to make life the best it can be. And not just for ourselves, but for everyone. For "one and all", because ultimately, the all *is* One.

A quote commonly credited to Mahatma Gandhi says it best:

"Be the change you wish to see in the world".

Love everyone and everything you encounter, so everyone and everything loves you. Make Love your religion.

There are many ways we can accomplish positive change, and several will be covered in later parts of this book, but perhaps the simplest way is to be kind and friendly and loving to every person and thing we encounter. Treat others as we wish to be treated.

Which brings us to rule #3.

Rule #3: *If someone or something from rule #2 causes you harm, refer to rule #1.*

As we all know, there are unfortunately those individuals who take advantage of kindness and love and friendship. We've all had that friend who was always around when *they* needed help, but were suddenly unavailable when *we* needed help. And also, we've all had someone who loved us as long as we were behaving in the ways they approved, but gave us "the cold shoulder" when we behaved in ways they disapproved. We've all had someone who loved us for *what we did for them*, rather than loving us for Who We Are.

So please remember this:

If you give, expecting something in return, it's not really giving at all.
If you love, expecting something in return, it's not really loving at all.

There is certainly value in (judiciously) allowing second chances to those who cause us harm. There is also power offered through apology, and healing provided through forgiveness. It may be naïve, but I am eternally hopeful that people who misunderstand or try to misuse love will eventually learn from their mistakes, and that will bring about change. But while that happens, while we wait, while we try to bring light into the darkness, love yourself and keep yourself from harm. Love freely, but never allow yourself to be treated like a doormat. Love yourself, love others, and dismiss those who would abuse you, use you, or harm those you love. Make your journey through life a magical adventure of Life, encountering Life.

Chapter 3 -- Unconditional Love

What is conditional love?

Conditional love is an oxymoron.
Conditional love is an imposter of love.
Conditional love is something other than love,
because you cannot conditionalize the un-conditional.

As it's been said: "Love is a many splendored thing". Love is kind. Love is patient. Love is giving. Love does not covet. Love is never arrogant, nor is it self-serving. Love is bliss, and Love is a powerful force.

There are few things in life that can end love, but there is nothing faster at ending love than *expectations*. Whenever someone expects a loved one to act a certain way, or dress a certain way, or behave a certain way, or perform certain tasks, they are conditionalizing their love. They are tacitly saying: "I will only love you so long as you do (X)". And this conditionalizing ultimately breeds resentment. What begins as a simple annoyance (he expects me to fix supper… or… he expects me to drag out the trash) can become bitterness, and bitterness can turn to anger, and eventually resentment, and even hatred.

For most of us, the thought of loving someone without ever expecting anything from them is unimaginable and frightening. All too often we depend on our loved ones to handle certain tasks. But the question we must ask ourselves is: are they doing this because *they want to do it*, or because *we expect them* to do it? There is a fine line between the two.

When it comes to loving someone, the ultimate gift we can give them is freedom.

Think about it. How many times have you seen a person fall in love with someone, only to want to change that person? It strikes us with deep irony when a person falls in love with another person because of "Who That Person Is", only to try and change that person, and then no longer love their own creation.

Again, the ultimate gift we can give our loved ones is the freedom to be Who They Are.

I don't mind saying, loving someone without condition is not an easy undertaking. Because of life's sometimes crazy and chaotic schedule, and often because of societies' stereotyping, it's very easy to find ourselves expecting "the *hers*" to clean the house, or "the *hims*" to fix the car, or mow the lawn. I certainly can't speak for everyone, but I can say my wife and I struggled with this for years. Over our 30+ years of marriage, it was only her exceptional communication skills that saved us from ripping out each other's throats over something as petty as sweeping the floor, or how to hang the toilet paper, or how to squeeze the toothpaste. (I know a couple who went to the brink of divorce from an argument that started over ketchup vs. mustard on a bologna sandwich – yes, it's true).

Through communication, what my wife and I discovered was that we each have different thresholds for different tasks. I came from a small and somewhat quiet household, whereas she came from a large and lively family. Therefore, when I saw four plates in the sink, by my perception "the kitchen was messy", while by her perception "there weren't enough dishes yet to wash". What we learned was, when a certain task bothered us, rather than being angry *or expecting* the other person to do it, simply do that task. It's that easy: just do it. After all, wouldn't we be doing it if we lived alone? And is it really worth arguing or causing resentment over whether the laundry was done or the lamps were dusty? If "he" wants to go fishing, and "she" would rather they go visit yard sales, is it really worth an argument or creating resentment? Is there no room for compromise?

Life should be lived as a Cooperation rather than a Competition. As the old adage goes: "it's not whether you win or lose, but how you play the game." But many people don't get this. They want to operate life completely on their own, and compete with others who are struggling with the *same issues* that they encounter. They fail to recognize they are winning nothing, and losing everything, because they establish themselves as "alone" -- just "them against the world". As for me, I'll gladly "Co-Operate" my own life with my wife's (and hers with mine), because Life is much more enjoyable when shared with someone you love. And when you love without conditions or expectations, and have the freedom to be Who You Are, life is that much easier to enjoy.

Chapter 4 -- Love observing Love

If you Love all Life you observe, you will observe all Life will Love.

My favored way of connecting to my higher self and God is through sitting quietly in the woods and observing Nature while listening to that "small voice" inside (more on this later). I am blessed, in the sense that my wife and I live in a small home, nestled near the middle of 25 acres of rolling hardwoods, which is in the middle of a much larger woods, and eventually surrounded by farm fields. We have a front yard, a small pasture, and a wonderful garden plot, but much of our land is rolling forest with small ravines and streams.

Often, I simply enjoy and appreciate Nature from the rear deck on our home. But at other times, when I want deeper solace or feel an urge to nourish my spirituality, I'll walk through the woods and find a towering oak and nestle between the roots. I especially like finding such a tree (or comfortable hillside) near the small streams that cross our property. Often, I will gather an egg-sized stone, hold it in my palm, and imagine all of Life's negativity draining into the stone. Once complete, I thank the stone, carefully "cleanse" it in the stream, and return it to its place in Nature.

On a couple of these spiritual pilgrimages, I've found such peace and tranquility amid Nature that I was lulled into a nap. On one cold still day, while sitting at the base of a large pine, I awoke to find a fresh dusting of snow had fallen while I slumbered. And on one colorful autumn day, I awoke to find a squirrel foraging acorns scant inches from my feet (I'm not sure which of us was more startled). The point from this is:

Nature will teach us many lessons if we take the time to visit her classroom.

We will cover many of Nature's wonderful lessons later, but for now, Her lesson is simple:

If you appreciate and love all the Life you observe, you will observe that all Life can (and does) love.

Humans are not the only animals who face struggles and hardships during Life, and it's our challenge to recognize this. Nor are humans the only animals who seek companionship, acceptance, and Love. This is easily evident with the pets we hold dear. But when we go out amid Nature, when watching birds, and squirrels, and deer, it becomes even clearer. And how can we know that animals love?

Because….

Chapter 5 – The Language of Love

v

Love is the language that transcends all others.

In his book, *For One More Day*, Mitch Albom states:

"When you look into your mother's eyes, you know that is the purest love you can find on this earth."[vi]

For many of us, this is how love is. We first learned love from our parents, and later began to see love in others. Love is easy for us to recognize, because we all intuitively speak the language of love. We can see it, sense it, feel it, and translate its actions. It's ingrained into our being. Love is a part of us, and we are a part of Love. It's ubiquitous. It surrounds us each day. We need only to pause from whatever we're doing and look for it, and it's suddenly there.

About a week ago, I was reminded of that. After finishing some menial outdoor chores around the house and barn, I decided to take a walk through our woods and check the trails for fallen limbs. More than anything, I just wanted to go for a walk and spend a few moments communing with Nature before retiring inside the house for the evening. As I reached the creek at the rear of the property, I became aware that the temperature was beginning to drop, so when I stopped to look at the creek, I purposely picked a spot in a sunny clearing, so the sun would help warm me.

While I was standing by the creek, just silently observing and enjoying the warmth of the sun, I watched a small school of minnows swimming back and forth in one of the deeper pools. Near the creek, three squirrels were frolicking; chasing each other from limb-to-limb, or running in spirals up and down the trees. In the distance, in the pasture beyond the creek, a calf rubbed up against its mother. And in the trees, a pair of sparrows sat together with puffed-out feathers to fend off the cold.

As I looked around the woods, I suddenly realized many of the woods were dappled in sunlight. While walking to the creek, I hadn't really noticed them... the woods felt shadowy and cold. But now that I had stopped and was enjoying the sun's kiss of warmth, I could see the sunny spots were everywhere, and I was walking more often through light, than darkness.

In a way, this is how it is with love. When we go to an event such as a wedding or dance, where the focus is love and it permeates the air, love seems like a common part of day-to-day life, and being in the presence of love makes us almost hyper-aware of it. When we are enjoying Love's kiss and warmth, we can see it all around us. Yet while we actually pass through that same day-to-day life, following life's bidding to some destination, we get so caught up in handling life's details that we're oblivious to the abundancy of love that surrounds us.

When we look for love, it's suddenly there, in the birds huddling together on the branch, in the squirrels frolicking in the trees, in the herd of cattle grazing the nearby pasture.

When we look for love, we can find it.

Of course many people have been hurt by love, and chosen to close their hearts to it. Some are even blind to it -- "atheists of Love", so to speak -- refusing to see at all. There's no doubt that Love can be difficult and potentially painful, but please remember this:

Love is always a risk worth taking, because nothing in Life can bring us more comfort and joy than Love.

Love can find its way into an open heart easier than a closed one, so if you want to feel love, open your heart and let it in.

When you show others love, you are shown love. When you give love, you receive love.

So don't wait for others to love you. Don't love someone *"because He first loved me"*, be the first to Love. Or smarter even yet, don't just feel love, *Be Love (*we'll talk more about this later). For God is Love, and therefore loving is one of the most "Godly" acts you can do.

Love freely, give freely, smile freely, because nothing (or "no thing") in Life matters more.

Part 2: Fear

Chapter 6 – Fear is darkness

"All the roads of Fear lead to the same destination: one of hardship, heartbreak, and ultimate unhappiness." -- *The Divinity Factor*

Okay. Ready to leave the warm light of Love and venture into the cold darkness? No? Neither am I, but here we go.

I want to make a confession. When I started writing this book, and begin drafting rough layouts of how to align the different parts (Life, Perception, Love, etc.), I wanted to leave out the section on Fear. My goal was to put out a positive message that might help someone, somewhere, and even if this message only helps one or two people lead more positive lives, the effort of writing this book is worthwhile. But as I began writing the early stages, I realized Fear is a necessary part. Just like in life, including it in the book was a "necessary evil". Even though it's hard to find positive things to say about Fear, to really understand the value and heights of Love, we must also understand Fear. To escape Fear, we must be willing to face it. Because we cannot "let something go" that we refuse to touch. Perhaps this is a lesson *I needed to learn.*

This is how life works. Whenever we have any traceable hardship in life, it can always be traced back to a fear (or usually many fears). These do not have to be our own fears, hardships or struggles can be created by the fears of other people and spread.

Love and Fear are polar opposites. Love originates from the soul, while Fear and worries and insecurities originate in the mind. Love is Heavenly, while Fear is Earthly. Love is a gift from Above, Fear is a burden from below.

In my previous book, *The Divinity Factor*, I shared a simple example to help readers understand the juxtaposition between Love and Fear. Since it might be helpful, I'd like to share an edited and condensed version here.

Love contains no Fear, because the mere presence of Fear desecrates Love and makes it something less than pure. As an example, imagine you have two 5-gallon buckets. In one bucket you have 2 gallons of the purest possible water (Love). In the other bucket, you have 2 gallons of toxic waste (Fear). If you dip 1 gallon of toxic waste (Fear) and pour it into the pure water (Love), what do you now have?

Answer: Two buckets of toxic waste.

The purest form of Love – Unconditional Love -- never contains Fear. Metaphorically speaking, it's like the purest glacier water that can be found. When you have a cup of pure Love, and add a single drop of Fear (toxic waste), you now have something that is impure. You now have something diluted; something less than Unconditional Love.

Many of history's prophets and religious leaders have shared this message. As one example, in the Bible, John wrote:

*"And we have known and believed the love that God hath to us. God **is** love; and he that dwelleth in love dwelleth **in** God, **and God in him**. ... There is no fear in love; but perfect love casteth out fear: because **fear hath torment**. He that feareth is not made perfect in love."* -- 1st John 4: 16 & 18

As we move forward in this book, we'll continually refer back and "flesh out" Love and Fear. Each of them have their own pure state, and in the case of Love, that pure state is what we commonly refer to as "Unconditional Love". It is "Perfect Love" (as John puts it). It is a love that is not watered down with conditions.

Fear is slightly different. Fear also has its own pure state, but this is often difficult to summarize in a simple term. So to help, I'll share a simple analogy.

Imagine that a person is scuba diving, and they are exploring some underwater caves near the coastline of a tropical island. Now imagine that the diver bobs to the surface, and finds that they are inside a dark, yawning underground cavern. This diver, not knowing if the cave might have an entrance, turns off their headlamp to see if there are any openings or light entering the cavern, but finds that there are none, and there is only blackness. No light at all enters this cave. The darkness is so black that one can't see their own hand when holding it inches from their face.

This type of blackness might be comparable to Fear in its purest form. It is the absence of all "light" or hope. It is the darkness in which we can easily become lost.

But let's look at another analogy, from a more *emotional* standpoint.

Imagine you are driving down the highway, running 60 mph, and suddenly a truck pulls out right in front of you, and you absolutely know there is no time or way to stop and you are going to T-bone that truck.

The terror you feel during that split second before impact is pure Fear. There is "no light"; nothing in your mind *except* that Fear.

This is the closest we might come to understanding pure Fear.

There is another analogy of Fear I'd like to share, but before I do so, I'd like to remind you that *my path is not a better path, just a different path.* What I'm saying is, I'm not asking anyone to change their beliefs – instead, I'm merely sharing mine. If it rings true within your soul, then we share a belief. If not, that's okay because regardless of how similar we each are, we are also different, each following our own path, and this exact diversity is what fills our world with beauty. (We'll speak more about this later).

To me, the "Devil" described in the Bible is a *metaphor* for Fear. This goes hand-in-hand with a number of Bible scriptures, including the previous scripture from 1st. John. In it, "God is Love" and "perfect love casteth out Fear, because Fear hath torment" (just as God cast out "Satan", who torments and punishes those who follow him).

When I was a child and teen, I attended church. I enjoyed many of the activities at church, but during that time, I continually struggled with the concept of a "literal" devil. It simply didn't make sense to me. For one, if God was really all-knowing, why would he create an angel (Lucifer) *knowing* that this angel would eventually rebel against Him, and later create "sin" by tempting Eve in the garden, and even later turn many of God's own children against Him? Secondly, if God is truly all-powerful, why couldn't He simply destroy "Satan" (like he destroyed Sodom and Gomorrah and many other "enemies" in the Bible), because by not destroying "Satan", doesn't it imply He wanted "Satan" to steal away souls and later torture them in "Hell"? Third, if "Satan" is more powerful than the other "fallen" angels, where did he obtain his supernatural powers? Did God give him those powers? And if so, why would a "loving" God do such a thing? And finally, if God truly loved His children, how much sense did it make for Him to lock His children in a room (Earth) with a confirmed "child-molester" (Satan)? How could a God who was loving -- Love itself -- do such a thing?

None of it made sense.

For 20 or more years after I left the church, I struggled with the notion of a "literal" devil. And then, the synchronicity of Life kicked in. One day while watching a documentary, and hearing FDR's infamous quote *("The only thing we have to fear, is fear itself!")*, it suddenly just "clicked" and everything fell into place.

God is Love and "Satan" is Fear. And like Love (but unlike a *literal* "devil"), Fear does have purpose (thus, God doesn't destroy it). Fear is what keeps us from walking to the edge of a 1000 foot cliff and simply stepping off. Fear keeps us from driving 100 mph down the interstate. (For some, it may be the fear of a ticket, more than the fear of an accident). Fear keeps us from swimming through shark infested waters, or walking into a storm, or running headlong into a burning building. As Queen Latifah put it:

"Fear can be good when you're walking past an alley at night or when you need to check the locks on your doors before you go to bed, but it's not good when you have a goal and you're fearful of obstacles."[viii]

Fear holds us back.

Fear prevents growth, and keeps us from achieving our goals. It is filled with "torment" and upset and hardship.

In an article at Intouch.org, Charles Stanley states:

"Fear stifles our thinking and actions. It creates indecisiveness that results in stagnation. I have known talented people who procrastinate indefinitely rather than risk failure. Lost opportunities cause erosion of confidence, and the downward spiral begins."[ix]

Opposite to Fear, Love propels us forward. Love can cause us to swim through shark infested waters, or run into a storm or burning building. Love frees us, and helps us reach our fullest potential.

Fear keeps us from applying for that job, or auditioning for a part, or trying new things, while Love causes us to "casteth out" or lay aside our Fear. Fear closes doors; Love opens doors.

Like "God" and "Satan", Fear and Love are the "Yin and Yang" of Life. They are the Light and Darkness. Our challenge is to know when to follow our fears (like not stepping off a cliff) and when to overcome Fear with Love.

Over the next few pages, we'll begin that journey.

Chapter 7 – Fear as a tool

"Many people do not want to forfeit their fears. Fear is the only tool they know."
-- The Divinity Factor

Now here's the funny thing about Fear. As a people, we relish it. From roller coaster rides, to haunted houses, to horror movies, to suspense thrillers, to bungee jumping or skydiving, we enjoy the effect of immersing ourselves in Fear. We love the rush it brings us, and how facing potential death makes us feel more alive.

For many people, Fear is a tool. It can be used to insure money in offering plates, or serve as a potent form of marketing. It is used for intimidation, or in discipline to discourage certain behaviors. It is a formidable weapon, and for many it is a useful tool.

In other cases, people who feel fears and insecurities, use Fear in their own lives. They use Fear to create ongoing drama in their lives, and this is how they keep their own lives poignant and interesting for themselves and others. These people usually believe that without some source of drama or crisis, their lives would be dull and dreary, and they *fear* that hum-drum. They *fear* that their lives are so lackluster and insignificant, that their friends and family might forget them, so in order to stay in the spotlight, they continually create drama around themselves.

And often what we see is, if you try to step in and solve whatever problem is causing the crisis or drama, these people will find reasons to discourage solving the problem, because they know that once the problem is solved, they lose the attention. *Or*, and this is often very telling, solving the problem they currently face will only create some new larger problem (i.e. – I'm sick and I need to take off work, but if I take off work, my power will be cut off Friday).

This is not to say that people don't face real struggles in life, because we do. It's a part of life. Good and bad times come and go; only change is certain. But we must be aware that some people *prefer* living in the darkness. They even create their own darkness. *Many people do not want to forfeit their fears. Fear is the only tool they know.*

Chapter 8 – Fear's reflection

You can either choose to walk in light and love, or run in fear and darkness. But with the latter, you're more likely to fall.

Okay. It's time to move on through Fear so we can return to the Light and cover more inspiring topics.

As we go through life, we feel a myriad of emotions. At times, we are on top of the world; at other times, we feel the weight of the world on us. We have moments we feel abandoned. We have flashes of angst and anxiety. We feel anger, astonishment, betrayal, befuddled, confused, content, delighted, distraught, disturbed… and these are only a few. There are literally hundreds of different emotions, some we can't even label or name. There are days for all of us when we have such poignant emotions coursing through us, it's difficult to define exactly what we are feeling.

It can all be overwhelming.

And this is where Love and Fear enter the picture.

I know it may seem incredibly simplistic, but every emotion we feel is based on the intensity of Fear or Love we feel regarding any particular subject, person or event, etc.. And sometimes, it is a blend of the two. It can even be a blend of two (or more) Loves and two (or more) Fears.

On one hand, it's almost overly simple, yet on another, it can be exceptionally complicated.

Let me expand a bit to help.

Some of our emotions -- such as being afraid, fearful, anxious, feeling terror, cowardly, or worried -- can easily be connected back to a specific fear. For example, if a person is afraid of a bully, they might act cowardly around the bully because of their fear of him or her. A person who is afraid of heights would feel fear if they near a cliff, and these emotions are easy to connect to Fear.

Other emotions, such as regret, sorrow, remorse, or guilt, aren't directly connected to Fear, but nonetheless can be traced back to it with a little effort. For example, let's pick "guilt" from that (partial) list. When we feel "guilt", we feel "guilty" because at some level we *fear* we did something wrong or harmful.

As you begin to understand this, it becomes evident that even emotions we don't directly connect with Fear are ultimately based in (or on) Fear.

Anger might be one such example. *Anger is Fear, expressed.* It is the mirror image of any fear we feel. When something threatens to physically or *emotionally* harm us (or someone/something we love), it makes us angry. But this anger begins as fear of that threat, and then is expressed outwardly as anger.

I'm going to repeat that for emphasis.

Anger is the mirror image of fear. It begins as fear, and is expressed outwardly as anger.

For instance, imagine you're sitting on the couch in a dark room, watching a horror flick, and just as the villain reaches the closet where protagonist is hiding, someone sneaks up behind you and yells "Boo!". At first, we feel a flicker of stark terror, but that terror quickly turns to anger towards whomever scared us. We express our Fear through anger. It is a natural survival response and part of the "fight or flight" *instinct*. We immediately feel anger, and adrenaline fuels our ability to protect ourselves. Now if we turn around and find out it was our giggling 5-year-old nephew who scared us, the anger quickly fades, because we realize the fear is unfounded and there is no real threat to our safety.

Here's another example. Imagine there's a couple, and the husband likes to go fishing on many Sunday mornings. Now imagine that the wife gets irritated with the husband because she would prefer he go to church. This makes the husband feel anger and resentful because he *fears* that she's forcing him to give up something he enjoys. The wife's irritation stems from her *fear* that the husband doesn't want to spend time with her, doesn't believe in her religion, won't consider her religion, or several other possible fears.

If you're adept, you're probably noticing a pattern here. All of the "darker" negative emotions stem from Fear. And the more we are exposed (and re-exposed) to any particular fear, the greater in intensity the emotion becomes. Petty annoyance becomes irritation, irritation becomes anger, anger becomes loathing, loathing becomes hatred.

Darkness gains its power from Fear. Light gains its strength from Love.

All the roads of Fear lead to the same destination: one of hardship, heartbreak, and ultimate unhappiness.

But there is hope....

Chapter 9 – Light overcomes darkness

At the heart of all anger, all grudges, and all resentment, you'll always find a fear that hopes to stay anonymous.

Okay. So now that we've talked about Fear, how do we overcome it? How do we cope with it?

First, let's talk briefly about the "lighter emotions".

Opposite to Fear, all positive emotions we feel – cheer, delight, enthusiasm, generosity, gratitude, etc., -- descend from Love, and are gifts from above.

I should mention, again, that – aside from *Pure Fear* and *Unconditional Love* – all other emotions are a blend of Fear and Love. *Even though the water is clear, it's not necessarily pure.* And again, they may be a blend of several Fears and Loves.

Take sympathy for example. Every time we see ASPCA commercials and hear Sarah McLachlan's angelic-yet-forlorn voice, it can "stir our emotions". We feel a blend of fear for animals that are being abused or abandoned, while also feeling a love for them. We fear their suffering may continue, and we want to support them and end their suffering. We feel a mixture of love and fear.

Hope is another example. With hope, we feel a love and desire for one outcome, despite fearing that other outcomes may occur. We're in a "black cave", but can see a faint light in the distance.

"Indifference" is another example, and helps in understanding the *intensity* of emotions. With indifference, we essentially feel no Love or Fear regarding the subject at hand. Complete and utter indifference is essentially the starting point of all emotions. It's the absence of emotion, because we feel neither Love nor Fear.

So here's the thing. To overcome our fears, we must first learn how to recognize and identify them. We must learn if they serve us (not walking off a cliff), or if they don't. And once we can put a name to our fear -- shine a light at it -- it suddenly loses all power. Light vanquishes darkness. The moment we know what it is, and can appreciate it for what it is, we take away its influence.

But there's a more important lesson to understand. The next time you find yourself in that black cave, or in the darkness, remember this.

Light always overcomes darkness.

"Darkness cannot drive out darkness: only light can do that. Hate cannot drive out hate: only love can do that." – Martin Luther King Jr., [xii]

Regardless of how dreary or black a cave might be, a single tiny light creates a space where darkness cannot exist. The light vanquishes the darkness. Try as it might, the darkness cannot conquer the light.

So the question we must ask ourselves is:

"Will we shine our light in the world, or simply be more darkness?"

That choice faces each of us in every action we take, and every decision we make. And as we make each decision, we must always ask ourselves: "does this choice provide the highest possible outcome?".

If you want to be someone who brings more light into the world … a "Bringer of the Light", let this be in your thoughts:

*Who are we?
We are nameless.
We are faceless.
We thrive in anonymity.
We are the stranger who smiles without reason.
We are the person ahead of you who pays your toll.
We are the diner who always tips.
We are the volunteers at the shelter.
We are the friend during time of need.
We are warriors for the planet.
We are pacifists for peace.
For we have looked, and saw.
For we have heard, and listened.
We walk through a world of darkness, bearing a message of Light and Love,
lighting the candles of those we meet.
We are the Bringers of the Light.
This is Who we choose to Be,
This is Who We Are*

Part 3: Perception

Chapter 10 – Looking for goodness

"It's been said that people see what they want to see. For that exact reason, look for the good in people, rather than the bad."

As you can see, this quote is akin to the story I shared earlier about noticing the sun-dappled spots on the forest floor. If you're in the forest and begin looking for puddles of sunlight, you will see them. If you look for patches of shade, you will see them. *What we look for is exactly what we will see.*

And we will believe exactly what we see. As it's frequently said: "seeing is believing".

But what many people don't realize is, while "seeing is believing", the exact opposite is also often true:

Believing results in seeing.

Let me give you a brief example, so you can understand what I mean:

In the 1400's, Man believed the world was flat and the sun revolved around the Earth. Because of this belief, Man developed a system of astronomy that mapped the locations and movements of the sun and stars that actually supported and re-affirmed Man's belief that the world was flat. He "saw" exactly what he believed, and even his science backed up what he was "seeing".

In much the same way, over the centuries many of Man's religions have taught that Man is "stained" or "blotched" by default. The problem with this thinking is, when people believe others are "stained by default", they will see exactly what they are looking for. They will look past a dozen virtues to find that one tiny sin that confirms their belief. They will overlook a sunny meadow to see a patch of shady darkness in the distance. (Seek, and you will find).

Contrary to this, when you believe people are pure and innocent from birth, the first thing you see is that purity.

So the question is, when we meet someone new, do we want to condemn or commend? Should we appraise, or simply praise? Do we reprove, or approve? Do we look for sin, or look within?

Which choice provides the higher outcome? What would Love choose?

Because whichever choice a person makes is a statement of Who They Are.

People who judge others tell more about Who They Are, than Who They Judge.

Racism is another perfect example of people seeing exactly what they look for. When people encounter others from a different race, and believe certain stereotypes about that race, they will see exactly what they believe. They will see whatever they are looking for.

Have you noticed that Man is the only animal that teaches racism?

What does Nature teach us?

Read on.

Chapter 11 – The beauty of color

xiii

Autumn teaches us a valuable lesson. During summer, all the green trees are beautiful. But there is no time of the year when the trees are more beautiful than when they are different colors.
Diversity adds beauty to our world.

Think about how bland our world would be without vibrant color. Yes, we can appreciate the odd skeletal beauty of the bare trees during winter, and blooming branches in spring, and the verdant and deep greens during summer, but autumn is a season to behold. Autumn allows us to see and appreciate every beautiful color the world has to offer. It helps us to understand our world is more beautiful with a variety of colors, than without it.

Remember when I said: "My path is not a better path, it is simply a different path?

Consider this similar affirmation:

My race is not a better race, it is simply a different race.

In Life's forest, we are each different leaves. Some are fiery red, some are sun yellow, some are brown, some are green, some are tan, and some are black. But beneath the colors, we are all leaves. We are a part of what makes the forest a forest. We are each a part of the whole.

("I am the vine, ye are the branches..." – John 15:5, KJV*).*

To rid the world of racism, we must help others understand this message. We must help others understand that although we may be different on the surface (pigmentation and minor feature differences), we are ultimately the same. We are all God's children, and we are each a part of the whole. We are all made from the same "stuff", and that "stuff" is the divine energy of God.

"For the body is not one member, but many. If the foot shall say, Because I am not the hand, I am not of the body; is it therefore not of the body? And if the ear shall say, Because I am not the eye, I am not of the body; is it therefore not of the body? If the whole body were an eye, where were the hearing? If the whole were hearing, where were the smelling? But now hath God set the members every one of them in the body, as it hath pleased him." – 1 Corinthians 12: 14-18, KJV

And consider this from the Bahai teachings:

"Since We have created you all from one same substance it is incumbent on you to be even as one soul, to walk with the same feet, eat with the same mouth and dwell in the same land, that from your inmost being, by your deeds and actions, the signs of oneness and the essence of detachment may be made manifest. Such is My counsel to you, O concourse of light!" – The hidden words of Baha'u'llah, #68[xiv]

Whether or not you realize it, Mankind is currently on a pathway to Oneness. It's a very long and arduous journey, and how fast we arrive *all depends on us*. Our journey is to return to God, and to accomplish that, we must first erode all the things in life that divide us. We must learn to recognize points of division and vanquish them. Because only when we see ourselves as part of the same vine, rather than separate vines, can we reach Oneness.

Let me provide an example so that's not so vague. Hundreds of years ago, women were viewed as "property" (and still are in some third-world countries). Over a number of centuries, women were eventually recognized as "individuals", but were still perceived as "inferior" to men. As we entered the 1920's, women eventually gained the ability to vote, becoming slightly closer to "equal" but still "less". Over the late 1900's the Feminism movement made further progress. Recently, in modern times, although we are still fighting for equal pay for women, more and more women are filling roles as leaders, business owners, CEO's, priests (and perhaps soon even President). The gender gap is slowly closing.

But this isn't the only side of gender discrimination. While women are drawing nearer to being seen as equals, the gay movement and the increasing societal acceptance of male/male and female/female relationships is decreasing the division Man sees in gender. To return to God (who is genderless), we must first become more like God by removing our stigmas about gender. And to accomplish this, we are slowly "de-gendering". It is but one step of many of Mankind's journey to return to God.

As our right foot has been stepping over the boundaries of gender, our left foot is beginning to step over racism. But that step is incomplete. We are far from ending bigotry, bias and racism. To accomplish this, Mankind must rethink and examine his ideals about perfection, superiority, and inferiority.

To help along the process, one thing we can do is speak out against racism or bigotry. Speaking out may help, especially if it's done diplomatically and with great compassion, but to ultimately change any undesirable behaviors we see in the world we must change the thinking that leads to those behaviors.

Let me repeat that for emphasis:

To change undesirable behaviors we see in the world, we must change the thinking that leads to those behaviors.

To help progress our return journey back to God, we must help people draw new perceptions and beliefs about whether racism and bigotry serve Mankind or only hinder our journey. We must help them understand that ultimately we are all One --- all of the same "body" (of God) and made from the same "stuff" (that is God), and no part of the body of God is superior or inferior to another part of God. Every part is essential, because every part contributes to the greatness of God.

Chapter 12 – Imperfect perfections

xv

"Every snowflake is unique, yet they are each perfect."

As you can see through this quote, Nature (which is God expressed) is teaching us a lesson about uniqueness and perfection. It teaches us that perfection and being different are not mutually exclusive. Each flake of snow is part of the larger body of snow. Each flake is individual and unique, yet part of the whole. Billions and billions of snowflakes may fall during a storm, yet which is imperfect? Is there one "perfect" snowflake that has fallen while all the others are flawed?

Is there one drop in the ocean that is superior to all others?

Or consider another example Nature provides us:

Some trees grow straight, while others grow gnarled and twisted.

If each tree grows exactly as it's designed, are any imperfect?

Is the tall, straight, and sparsely-limbed tree that's "perfect" for a lumberjack also a "perfect" tree to someone who wants to build a treehouse? Will that tall, straight "perfect" tree also be the "perfect" tree for a swing?

What about a child born with Down's syndrome or missing a toe, is the child "imperfect", or is it "perfectly different"?

As we can understand from these rather simplistic examples, perfection is both subjective and relative.

Perfection is merely a perception.

The "perfect" man for one woman may not be the "perfect" man for another woman, and certainly not the perfect man for all women. "Imperfections" to one person may be perfections to another.

("Love your curves and all your edges, All your perfect imperfections." – John Legend, *All of Me)*

At first glance, perfection and racism seem to have no common connection, but they have a very important connection. To end racism, we must change the thinking that leads to racism. We must change the ideal that some people are superior (more perfect) to others, and some races are superior (more perfect) to others. We must eradicate the ideas of "superiority" and "inferiority", because they create division between Man and Man, Man and Woman, and Man and Nature. We must teach that perfection is *always* merely a matter of perception, and therefore, there is really nothing that is "superior" or "inferior", just things that are *different*.

But let's look at it a little differently:

Many years ago, a co-worker of mine came in to work one day, beaming. He had a two-year daughter, and she was truly the apple of his eye. He proceeded to tell me that the previous night she had sung for the very first time. He said:

"Don, she missed some of the words and some of the notes, but it was the most beautiful thing I've ever seen!"

I believe this is the way God looks at us, His children. During life, we may make some mistakes and often fall down or sing out of key, but it is still beautiful to God, because we are His children.

So never allow anyone to convince you that you are "imperfect", because "perfection" is always a perception. Perfection is a concept created by Man, and it is always subjective. To your parents, or your spouse, or someone, somewhere ... you are "perfect". Even with what Man considers "flaws", you were created by a perfect God to perform *exactly as He designed you*. Whether that be with a missing toe, or psoriasis, or anything else Man considers a "flaw", you were created exactly as you are, to learn a specific lesson or have a specific purpose during life. How much more "perfect" can it get?

Now let's move a step further and look at a different type of perception:

Many people say "Everything happens for a reason" when what they really believe is "some things happen for a reason". I would ask that you have the courage to believe the former. There is no such thing as luck, or coincidence, or chance. All events -- good or bad -- are part of a larger plan. Everything is a part of a greater synchronicity that occurs in life.

I know this can be a hard pill to swallow, because when "bad" things happen to us, they can leave us questioning the whole purpose and direction of our lives. But have you ever considered the possibility that the "bad thing" happened for that exact reason ... to make us question or rethink a certain choice or the current direction of our lives?

Chapter 13—Curves in the path

xvi

Never view obstacles in your path as the enemy. Rather, view any obstacles as detour signs to avoid pitfalls.

We've all been there. We've all had that day when it seems that Murphy's Law rules the universe and "what can go wrong, will go wrong". It's that day when you have a low tire on the car, and spend 15 minutes pumping it up with an ancient puttering portable air compressor, or easing the car to a nearby garage. And finally, after getting the tire repaired, we inevitably get caught behind a frequently stopping school bus, or stuck in bumper-to-bumper traffic. We all know how the day goes. In the rush to pick up our coffee, because we're hurrying from being late, we spill it down our shirt or blouse. Then we realize we've forgotten something important at home. And all this seems to happen when we have some important type of meeting scheduled. On those days, it feels like we're paying some karmic debt, or the universe is plotting against us.

In a way, perhaps it is. Perhaps a guardian angel or spirit guide or God is trying to prevent us from entering into some business deal that will eventually cause us to move, or have us away from home when an ill child needs us. Or, perhaps it's delaying us to ensure we'll be "at the right place, at the right time" to meet Mr. or Ms. "Right". Perhaps we *are* paying some type of karmic debt. Sometimes we just don't know the *whys*. Sometimes we never find out "why" something happened. But other times, we find out later that, had we entered such and such deal, it would have bankrupted us. Or had the car tire not been flat, we would have been on the 95th floor of the World Trade Center on the morning of September 11th, 2001.

When "bad" things happen, don't view them as negative, view them as God or Life sending you a detour to help you avoid larger pitfalls.

I have a little affirmation I like to tell myself on those "Murphy's Law" days:

A river has many curves, but it always reaches the ocean.

The flat tire on your car, that's going to make you late for work, may also be a "delay" to prevent you from being struck by a car that's going to run a red light in five minutes. The snowstorm that's preventing you from going to a party, may also be preventing you from catching the flu while at that party.

Just like perfection, "good" and "bad" are always relative or subjective. It's all a matter of our perception. It's all a matter of how we look at things. A rain storm may be "bad" to the little leaguers playing baseball, but "good" to the farmer living next door, who's been hoping for rain.

Everything is a matter of perception, and perception is everything.

Ultimately, we are the ones who decide what "good" and "bad" are. We decide what is "perfect" and "imperfect". We are the creators of our perception, and through that perception, we decide what life is.

But let's go one step further.

Happiness and Unhappiness are not things that just happen to you, they are a choice. They are a perspective.

Smile, and think about that for a moment.

Now smile some more.

Not that hard is it?

The irony is, some people spend a lifetime searching for happiness, or love, or joy when they already have all these (and much more) inside of them. We all already possess them, and have them in abundance. Despite Air Supply's hit song, we can never truly be "*All out of Love*". We simply cannot run out of love, or happiness, or joy. And we can experience them anytime we want simply by giving them to others. If you want to feel joy, go out and give someone a gift that will make them joyous and see how you feel. Want to laugh and be happy? Go out and make someone else laugh and be happy today and see what happens.

Chapter 14 – Creating good days

xvii

"A day is a day. It's just a measurement of time. Whether it's a good day or a bad day is up to you. It's all a matter of perception."

As you can see, this quote goes hand-in-hand with the last section. It's truly all a matter of perception. How we perceive each day, whether it's "good" or "Bad" is all up to us.

We are the "great deciders". No one else decides for us. So when we rush out the door to go to work and find a flat tire on our car, we have to recognize both the *negative* and the *positive* of the situation. Yes, it's going to slow us down and we may be late for work (the negative), but it may also be supernatural forces protecting us (the positive). Or it may be God *slowing us down* so we bump into a new client or meet our next best friend at the gas station. Even though we don't know the reason at that moment, there may be a very good reason why this "bad" is happening and creating a detour for us.

Here's a simple truth:

What happens to you during Life may seem out of your control; how you perceive each experience, however... good or bad... is totally up to you.

You can choose to live in chaos by "reacting" to whatever Life throws at you, or you can rearrange the letters, and choose "creating" what you throw at life. The choice is up to you.

Many people live a reactionary existence.

They go through life being controlled by other people (or circumstances) rather than controlling their own destiny. They allow others to say things or do things to "get a rise" out of them. And whenever the others do this, they react. Then the others react and they react to that reaction. And so on, and so on. They are being controlled by their reactions, and they are choosing to do this by *reacting* rather than *creating*.

Breaking the cycle requires changing and rearranging. Turn "reactions" into "creations".

Sometimes, the simple act of pausing to take a deep breath can hold miraculous power. Often, a pause is like putting on a pair of glasses, and suddenly being able to see Life more clearly. A simple pause can allow Life to deliver you a higher outcome. By pausing and taking a deep breath and objectively accessing the situation, you are *choosing* your next step – creating -- rather than just reacting.

As Garnet Schulhauser, author of *Dancing On a Stamp* and *Dancing Forever with Spirit*, once said:

"Every day is a new beginning--another opportunity to follow the path of light toward enlightenment."

So always remember: " *"A day is a day. It's just a measurement of time. Whether it's a good day or a bad day is up to you. It's all a matter of perception."*

Chapter 15 – The power of thought

xviii

Your words, your thoughts, your imagination: powerful tools. Remember that and use them wisely.

When was the last time you stopped to think about how often you think? I know that sounds funny, but it's easy to forget how often we use our brains each day. We get up in the morning and launch ourselves into the day's events, thinking about tasks as we go, but seldom acknowledge how much thought goes into each simple process. Thinking is something we take for granted... usually, right up until the time we make a mistake because "we weren't thinking".

In my own life, I can recall plenty of mistakes caused by "not thinking". As one example, one particular morning I got up, turned on the morning news, began fixing breakfast, and a few moments later arrived at the breakfast table only to realize I had a bowl of coffee-drenched cereal and a mug of cold milk. On another occasion, when we broke for lunch one day at work, I opened my lunch and discovered the mustard bottle neatly packed where my sandwich should have been (luckily, I had some snack crackers to eat).

We've all done it. We've all had that moment when we forget to grab our cell phone, or the charger, or our keys, or our coat, or a map, or some other item. We say that we "forgot" these things, when what we really "forgot" was to think.

And it's at these times when we're most aware of the value of thought (I should have thought of that!).

But this isn't the only time we value thought. Whenever we look at some new gadget or gizmo that fills us with wonder, we can appreciate both the thought and the imagination that went into creating whatever gadget or gizmo it is. In day-to-day life, we're surrounded with such wonders while barely giving them a second thought. Take a simple "AA" or "D" size battery for example. This small and compact product contains enough energy to power a camera, flashlight, remote controller, or a variety of other items for many hours of use. A wall clock is another example. Either wind it up or insert a battery (or two), and it can keep track of time for weeks, or even months.

As a young boy, I can recall feeling this type of awe and wonder towards many of the machines on my Uncle's farm. The hay baler was a great example. Hook it up behind a tractor, pull it around a field of raked hay, and it would gather the hay from the ground, pack it tightly into nice square bales, tie up the bale, and eventually push the neatly tied hay bale out a rear chute. I can remember one day, after my Uncle had finished working with the hay, carefully examining the hay baler and trying to figure out how it worked. To a young boy, it was a marvel.

The combine was another such wonder. Drive it around the soybean field, and it would cut off the plants, shell the soybeans from their pods, and deposit all the soybeans in a large storage bin while it also spit out the pulverized plants to use them as silage. It was an amazing machine, as were many of the machines and devices on the farm. And you could look at them and see the thought and imagination that had gone into creating them.

All of the great inventions we enjoy in modern life are born through the power of imagination and thought, combined with creativity. All of our plays and movies, the cars we drive, the homes where we live, the songs we sing and listen to, and the devices that play these songs are each products of the power of imagination and thought.

And we each hold this power.

But we can't "forget" words. Our words are also powerful. They have the ability to harm or heal, and are the building blocks of thoughts. It's akin to a child who has a set of "ABC" blocks, and slides the "C", "A", and "T" blocks together to spell "CAT". A thought may start as a single word and become something much larger and greater. Hearing a simple word like "beach" may fuel our imagination, and have us thinking of whether we can afford a trip, and find the time.

But let's look at words, thoughts, and imagination in a different light:

Suppose a person is at home, alone, sitting in their living room and watching TV and out of the corner of their eye they see a shadowy form pass by a doorway. Was it a shadow? A ghost? Or the light playing tricks on their eyes? A bit unsettled, they resume watching TV, but are slightly more aware of that doorway. Then another shadowy figure passes the doorway. This time they jump up and investigate, checking the entire house and looking outside to see if the shadow was caused by someone walking past a light.

Finding no one in the house and nothing outside that might have caused a shadow, the person believes they may have just seen a ghost. That is their experience, and it was very real for them. Their experience was "seeing a ghost". If they didn't previously believe in ghosts, this experience changes "what Life is and means". It becomes a part of Who They Are.

(Again, seeing is believing... yet believing may also result in seeing).

As you can see from this same example, if the person who sees the shadow already believes in ghosts, they'll reach the conclusion that the shadow was a ghost much sooner. They may not even bother to check outside.

Our words and our thoughts and our imagination are very powerful tools, because they help form our perceptions, and our perceptions then form our beliefs of *what is real*, *what an experience meant*, and ultimately *what Life is and means*. These perceptions eventually become our reality and our memories. They form Who We Are from the ground floor up.

Chapter 16 – Soaring with imagination

xix

Money can take you many places, but imagination can take you anywhere.

Thoughts have the power to shape our perceptions and reality, and words form the thoughts and let us convey the thoughts to others, but imagination can literally take us to places we can only *imagine*. In your imagination, you can do or be anything. In an instant, you can be relaxing on the beach, or be young again and skipping across a grassy meadow, or be a superhero, or visit the moon, or endless other possibilities.

In imagination, you can even create imaginary friends and people. You can do or *be* anything you want.

But beyond just serving as a retreat from Life, imagination can be a powerful resource. We can use it to envision new tools, or machines, or vehicles, or new systems for performing tasks. Imagination is the author of many arts, and works of fiction, and new games, or movies or plays. *No author has ever been more prolific than Imagination.* It fuels our dreams, and can impact our future.

Through artistry, imagination not only allows one to express their creativity, but also their soul.

But like all things, imagination can also be used for "bad". While we can imagine having an imaginary best friend who loves us unconditionally, the same imagination can create a monster hiding under the bed or living under bridges, or lurking in the darkness.

Imagination is a powerful tool, with many powerful uses.

"I believe that imagination is stronger than knowledge. That myth is more potent than history. That dreams are more powerful than facts. That hope always triumphs over experience. That laughter is the only cure for grief. And I believe that love is stronger than death." – Robert Fulghum[xx]

Superstitions are a suitable example of the power of thought and imagination at work. Superstitions have power, but only the power you give them. They can bring good luck (like finding a 4-leaf clover or catching the bride's bouquet) or bad luck (which may also be catching the bride's bouquet). What they bring is up to you. You are the "great decider".

To some people, crossing the path of a black cat is a harbinger of "bad luck", and to people who believe this, they will experience "bad luck" if they look for it long enough. Again, *seeing is believing, and believing can result in seeing*. If this person crosses the path of a black cat and is watching for "bad luck", they will see exactly what they are looking for, and may even attract negative energy ("bad luck") to their lives.

Our society has numerous superstitions, ranging from walking under a ladder, to stepping on a crack, to breaking a mirror, and hundreds of other examples. I chose to use the black cat example for a specific purpose. Here in the U.S., walking across the path of a black cat supposedly brings bad luck. And here, black cats are often linked to being witch's familiars. Yet in other cultures black cats signal success. According to Wikipedia[xxi], many of the Scottish believe that if a black cat shows up on your porch, you will come into unexpected riches. In Japan, a black cat is good luck, while in Germany, if a black cat crosses your path from left to right, it's bad luck, but if the cat crosses from right-to-left, it's good luck. As you can see, it's highly unlikely that a black cat is "bad luck" in the U.S., yet would become "good luck" if the same cat were transported to Japan.

To me, seeing a black cat cross my path simply indicates the cat is going somewhere. It is moving. It's that simple.

I do not believe in "luck", or "chance", or "coincidence". But nor do I wish to impose my beliefs onto anyone else. I simply present them as they are. If they ring true to your soul, you have found something new and valuable. If not, dismiss what you don't believe and embrace what you do. As always, my path is not a better path, it is just a different path.

If a person chooses to believe in luck, that's fine. That may be part of their path. What I would simply encourage is that:

If you believe in "luck", always let it be good luck.
Always choose to be "lucky", rather than "luckless".
Be "happy", rather than "hapless".

Everything else falls into place.

Give to Life exactly what you wish to receive back.

And above all, remember this:

Happiness is truly priceless. It costs you nothing.

Part 4: Life

Chapter 17 – The party of life

Life is like a 6-slice apple pie at a 12-guest dinner banquet. If you just sit back and wait for it to come to you, chances are, you're going to miss dessert.

As you've gathered by now, I love Nature. I'm sure that will show even more when we reach the next section of this book (Nature). I love walking in the woods and being surrounded by Nature. And even while I write this from within the cozy comfort of my home, I can turn and gaze out the window and see the beckoning woods nearby.

The thing about the woods and Nature is, it's a lot like day-to-day life. The woods today appear the same as they did a week ago. And if I glance out the window again tomorrow, it'll be much the same. Yet over time, the woods is constantly changing and evolving. A pine that once towered over the hardwoods has fallen, and within the ridge of decaying bark and trunk, saplings are sprouting up amid the rich loam left by their "parent". The hickory "grocery" for the squirrels has been replaced by a holly "bed and breakfast" for the birds. And in a few months, the cold, still nights of winter will give way to the wet spring morning showers, and the denizens of Nature will emerge from their homes, and busy themselves with life, only stopping to rest in the hot and redolent afternoon of summer. And come the evening of autumn, after the work is done and provisions have been gathered, they head back into their dens and prepare for another night of winter.

In a lot of ways, the life faced by Nature is similar to our own. There are periods of illness and suffering, and times of health and abundance. There are some who have stockpiles, and others who go starving. There are mates that come and go, and others who become partners for life. There are days of fair and pleasant weather, and nights of windy storms. And just as we each face this in our own lives, we must realize humans are the only animals who suffer to survive.

During life, many people see themselves as hapless victims. They feel they must endure whatever obstacles or hardships life hurls toward them. They live constantly reacting, and rarely creating. They sit back at Life's dinner table, waiting for someone to pass the pie, only to learn it's gone. Then they often complain or feel self-pity afterwards.

Others compete for it. They try to snatch up the largest slice, without thinking of those who go hungry. They view life as a competition… he with the most toys wins… and have difficulty perceiving cooperation as a higher outcome.

Those who are creative and giving have a different approach. Split each piece of pie into halves, and suddenly a 6-slice pie feeds 12. The slices may be smaller, but everyone gets to enjoy. And tomorrow, at the next dinner, everyone will enjoy again.

The thing about life is, when we make it about conquests and failures, there are winners and losers. But when we make it an act of cooperation, there are only winners.

Life isn't about climbing a mountain, and saying "There. That's it. I've done it!" Life is about climbing a mountain, and knowing there are many more mountains to climb.

Life isn't about finding the answers, life is about knowing there are always more questions.

Chapter 18 – Life nurtures

If you nurture Life, Life will nurture you.

Just as a clarification, allow me to point something out. When I refer to "life" as "the event we all go through", it is un-capitalized. It's simply "life". Yet when referring to "some, or all things living", "Life" takes on a sacred connotation and deserves the recognition of capitalization. It is a "proper" noun. I'm not suggesting it's "proper" grammar, but it's none-the-less proper. It is simply part of my path.

Now let's move on.

We all know the ubiquitous quote: "*Stop and smell the roses*". It's cute, yet trite, and there is a great deal of truth behind it. All too often, we get so caught up in the day-to-day ritual of our lives that we forget to stop and notice Nature's beauty that surrounds us. We fail to make our lives a *"magical journey of Life, encountering Life."*

But that magical journey is more than just stopping to sniff a pot of fragrant flowers, or watching squirrels frolic in the trees. We must nurture Life too. We must not just smell the plants or revel in their beauty, we must water them. We must feed them. Nurture them. So when you return to them again, they're as bright and brilliant as ever.

Again, humans are not the only animals who suffer to survive. When we "split the pie" and share, there are more winners than losers.

But nurturing life goes far beyond this. You must nurture your own life too. And the lives of others. And consider the idea that the two are not mutually exclusive.

Regardless of what you are doing with your life, you are making a difference. Whether or not you realize it, every action, every re-action, or every non-action impacts Life. So the question to ask yourself is not whether you are making a difference, but whether that difference is positive or negative.

What have you done today to help yourself? What have you done today to help others?

Chapter 19 – Be a master

*"Seek to be served, and you become a servant.
Seek to serve others, and you become a master."*

Okay, I know that quote sounds counter-intuitive. After all, isn't a master someone who *has* servants and is served? And isn't a servant someone who serves others? Isn't this completely backwards?

In short, the answer is "no".

How can that be?

Let's back up for a moment.

When you give love, you receive love.
When you give joy, you receive joy.

Now let's add to that:

When you serve others, you are served.

Still not sure? Okay, bear with me as I explain in more depth.

Some of our businesses primarily sell products (i.e. Walmart, Macy's, etc.). Other businesses focus on selling services (i.e. tax preparers, maids, attorneys, designers, etc.). And even others sell a combination of both products and services (i.e.

restaurants, car dealerships, cell phone provides).

Now let's assume that "Andrew" decides to open a service-oriented company. He wants to create websites for his customers. And in doing so, Andrew wants to focus on giving his customers the best possible website at the most competitive price. His goal may be to make money and earn a living, but while doing that, Andrew also wants to give his clients the best service possible. Impeccable service is important to Andrew.

Next, let's assume that because of the high quality and low prices of Andrew's web-page building service, his business is a hit. His customers refer others, and they also return to him whenever they need updates or newer websites. As a result, Andrew becomes so successful that he needs to hire more and more help. And as the years pass by, Andrew continues to offer high-quality low-price websites, and his business continues to blossom and grow. Because of the reliable and affordable service he offers, Andrew becomes successful. He becomes "a master" through the repetitive service he gives others, because, when his customers have future needs, who do they turn to? They turn to the "master" who can fulfill those needs. The customers may perceive themselves as the master (because they are being served), and Andrew as the "servant", but the roles have actually reversed even though the perceptions haven't yet caught up. Through repetitiously serving others, Andrew has reached a point where others serve him.

Of course, the example of Andrew is very *materialistic* and *capitalistic* oriented, so let's stop and look at being a master in a more *spiritual* manner, and then we'll move to a more "day-to-day" model.

All of history's great spiritual leaders have understood that the greatest and highest action they can do is to serve others. If you think about it, this is what Jesus did. He didn't put down roots and try to acquire wealth, instead, he roamed the region, healing people, feeding others, and teaching (*give, and it shall be given unto you*). His goal was to serve God and serve others. He often washed the feet of others. And through serving God and others, he became a master.

Siddhartha, who is better known as The Buddha, followed a similar path. Siddhartha's father was a king, and Siddhartha, being a prince, was born into a life of wealth and splendor. For the first 28 years of his life, Siddhartha spent nearly all his time confined within opulent palaces. But while he had all the things necessary to live lavishly, Siddhartha couldn't find emotional or spiritual fulfillment. He didn't understand how people outside the palace walls lived in a deplorable state of continual suffering, while those inside lived in luxury. He had many questions that were unanswered.

When he turned 29, Siddhartha commissioned one of his chariot drivers to take him on a day-tour (of sorts) outside the palace and around the area, and during this trip, for the first time in his life, he encountered the reality of human suffering and frailty. Upon seeing a very old man, the charioteer explained to Siddhartha that all people age. And beyond seeing many elderly, they also encountered people who were diseased and starving. Later in the day, they saw a monk, and the chariot driver explained to Siddhartha that monks had chosen to reject worldly possession so that they could travel the region and help people cope with the fear of death, and alleviate suffering.

Moved by this experience, Siddhartha left home the next day, and set out to become a monk and help those who suffered. For 6 years, he tagged along with a small group of monks, practicing with them. When he wasn't with the monks, he sought enlightenment by fasting or meditating while seated beneath a Bodhi tree (which later became known as "the Wisdom tree"). Over time, people began visiting Siddhartha, and would frequently ask him to meditate and seek an answer for whatever hardship they were presently enduring. When they returned, Siddhartha (who soon became known as "The Buddha") would share whatever wisdom he learned during meditation. Through serving others, Siddhartha became a master.

Upon seeing Buddha's example, many monks and spiritual leaders began practicing meditation beneath trees within villages, and often near the doors of shops where villagers would come-and-go. The monks and spiritual leaders learned that, by being in more visible and frequented areas, they could reach and serve more people. The swamis of Hare Krishna especially embraced this, and over time, began setting up at airports, parks, and shopping centers.

And this principle holds true in day-to-day life. When you volunteer at a food kitchen or shelter, you become the "master" through serving others. You are who they look to for deliverance from their suffering. When you continually make yourself available to serve others, they turn to you.

Remember, your thoughts and words are powerful tools, and whatever thoughts you send out will manifest and return to you. When you continually tell Life: *"there are things that I lack and things that I want"*, Life will return that <u>exact</u> experience. You can never be free to truly have others "serve you", because all your time and effort is focused toward serving yourself… fulfilling your own wants… being a "servant" to yourself. But when you continually tell Life: "*I have all that I need and am free to serve others*", Life will return that exact experience: you will have all you need and will be free to serve others.

As you can see, we are beginning to compound our lessons here. When you give love (by serving others), you receive love. When you show love, you are shown love. When you give joy, you receive joy. When you give happiness, you receive happiness. And when you give respect to others through serving them, you receive respect. By default, you are on the path to becoming a Master through your service. You gain love, joy, happiness and respect because you *give* them. You have all the things you need in life because you tell Life you have these things and are free to serve others.

Chapter 20 – To Be or not to Be

You cannot be a positive influence to the "sinners at the table" if you refuse to dine with them.

Okay. For a moment, it's going to seem like we're skipping over the above quote and talking about a different subject. As a matter of fact, it may seem that we're skipping from one subject to next, without much correlation existing between each subject. But rest assured that's not the case, and we'll pull this quote and everything else back into the conversation in the next few pages.

Remember when we spoke about the Fear having purpose… such as preventing people from walking off a 1000-foot cliff? I'd like to return to that example very briefly, in a scaled down manner.

When I was child, one of the neighborhood kids lived in a small house with several large leafy maple trees in the front yard. Each autumn, as soon as the leaves fell, myself and all the neighborhood kids would gather at this neighbor's house and chaotically rake the leaves into a huge pile. Once the pile was made, we'd take turns running and diving into it, riding our bicycles into the pile, hiding in the pile, fastening kites to our arms and trying to "fly" (and land in the pile), laughing and wrestling in the leaves, and all the inventive play that children do. As this progressed, we learned that we could also pile the leaves up and jump safely into the pile from the lower tree limbs. This gave us quite a thrill, and we soon began embracing our Fear and trying to "defy gravity" by jumping from higher and higher branches. That usually lasted until all of us had several scratches, and a couple of kids (and often myself) had sprained ankles.

The thing I'd like to point out is, this is another case of Nature and Life teaching a lesson. During those days playing with fluttering leaves, and jumping from the trees, we learned more about gravity than a year's worth elementary science class. But the most important lesson learned was that gravity does not pick favorites. It doesn't care what skin color you have or whether you're "good" or "bad". It doesn't care if you "respect" it and release yourself reverently from the limb, or you "defy" it and release yourself recklessly. Gravity does not "reward" or "punish", it simply does what God designed gravity to do as part of the universal laws of cause and effect. It's simply a matter of action and a predictable reaction. And it bears mentioning here that "action and reaction" is not the same as "choice and consequence". If a person is on the roof of a one-story house, and decides to step off (the action), the naturally occurring re-action is to fall. They may suffer an injury as a *consequence* of their decision, but it's not a case of gravity "punishing" them. Gravity simply does what it was designed to do.

As you may have guessed, I do not believe in the concept of "sin". But again, *my path is not a better path, it is simply a different path.* To me, the idea of a God who has to keep a "good/bad" checklist of each person is a very small idea of Who and What God Is. I believe that God is much larger, and has laid out a number of invisible universal "karma-like" laws that work similar to gravity. These laws do not "pick favorites". There is no preference as to whether a person is a Christian, or Wiccan, or Jew, or Muslim. Putting it as simply as possible, whenever a person acts with Darkness or Fear, they will receive in like kind. And whenever a person acts with Light or Love, they receive in like kind.

"Give, and it shall be given unto you... For with the same measure that ye mete withal it shall be measured to you again." – Luke 6:38 KJV

These laws are designed to help us learn and grow through the natural occurrence of life. Their purpose is to steer us toward Love without ever interfering with our Free Will. In the truest sense, life is a mirror, reflecting back exactly whatever we show it. It reflects your state of mind, echoing the words you use, expressing the ideas you hold, manifesting the actions you place in the world. Everything you send out returns to you. Do good… giving Love or Joy… and goodness returns to you. Be cruel to others, and they will be cruel to you. Be kind, and kindness returns to you.

It largely depends on how or what you are choosing to *be* at any given moment.

Always remember, Who You Are is not limited to your body. And Who You Are is not defined by What You Do. Who You Are is always determined by how you are choosing to *be*.

Let me expand on that. …

We are human-beings, not human-doings. When we decide to "be" a certain thing, the "doing" is a naturally occurring result. If we decide to become a surgeon, operations are a part of what a surgeon does. The "being" comes first and the "doing" naturally follows.

The Being/Doing concept has been shared many times in the past… even as far back in time as Shakespeare, who poised the question in *Hamlet: "To be, or not to be?"*. It's worth noting that the question isn't: "To do, or not to do?", but instead focuses on *being*.

The thing is, many people haven't grasped the fullness or breadth of *being*, and limit it to *occupations*. They think of *being* a doctor or being a policeman, but they don't think of *being* kindness or *being* love. And that's a hurdle we must overcome. We must understand that a person can *be* kind even though they work as a veterinarian and occasionally must euthanize animals. They can *be* generous even though they work as a debt collector.

Ultimately, the "being" will influence and correct the "doing". While a kind person may very well remain a veterinarian (and most I've met are very kind), a generous person probably won't work long as a debt collector. Either they will try to change the process, or the process will change them.

This is why we should always strive to *be* loving, and kind, and generous, and friendly, and quick to smile. Because being those things results in doing, and the doing results in "karma" returning to us actions of like kind.

This is not always easy. As we all know, there are "sinners at life's table" who can make it difficult. They can make you want to "be angry" or "be selfish" or "be" a number of other Fear-based *be*haviors.

As previously mentioned, some people believe "life is a competition" (rather than an event of co-operation). In their world, "he who has the most toys wins", and therefore, "it's every man for themselves". This provides them with the perfect justification for "being selfish" and throwing obstacles in the path of others, rather than helping others. The idea of "serving others" is counter-intuitive to them, and as a result, they spend a lifetime wishing to be a master, yet being a servant to themselves. They fully believe that through acquiring riches and belongings, they will become Masters. But they fail to see that their greed perpetuates their own slavery.

So here is a sound piece of advice…

Chapter 21 – Be the light

xxvi

Always let your inner light shine. By doing so, you not only light a path for yourself, but also light a way for others.

Whenever you love without condition, your light shines.
Whenever you give joy, your light shines.
Whenever you share happiness, your light shines.
Whenever you smile, your light shines.
Whenever you forgive, your light shines.
Whenever you help others, expecting nothing in return, your light shines.
Whenever you appreciate every person, and every part of creation, your light shines.

Doing these things let your light shine. But don't do them simply for the sake of being a light for others, do them because you understand these actions make you a higher version of Who You Are. Don't just carry a light, *be* the light. Be love. Be joy. Be happiness. Be forgiving. Be helpful. Be appreciative.

Never be afraid to let your inner light shine. Through the action of lighting a path for yourself, you will light a path for others.

It is, of course, desirable to all of us to "be the light" for others. After all, helping others is a part of keeping your own light shining brightly. And being a light… teaching others about love and happiness (etc.) is one of the most gratifying and fulfilling deeds we can accomplish during life. It not only enriches the other lives we touch, but it also embellishes our own life. And through being an example and light for others, we know we're brightening the world one light at a time. The more people we influence, the more darkness we banish. And through this process we make the world a brighter place.

This is another step in spiritual evolution that all masters know and practice. The success of a master is not measured by how many students they have, *but how many masters they create.*

We might return to the story of Andrew as an example. As Andrew grows his business, and trains employees, and eventually some of those employees become "managers" and "supervisors" and are able to train new employees, Andrew is creating "masters" who can "carry the torch" after he retires or moves on.

The same holds true for us. Always remember that with a single candle, you can light hundreds of other candles. So don't simply strive to have a large number of followers, instead strive to use your candle to light theirs, so they can use their candle to reach and light others.

Nature teaches us many valuable lessons. And we will cover some of Her lessons in a later section. But there's one particular lesson that applies here. At night, moths and fireflies and many nocturnal creatures are drawn to the light. Turn on a spotlight on your home and here they come. They crave it, as if it is the essence of Life. They long for the light.

But not all creatures seek the light. Some fear the light. Build a camp fire in the woods or meadow and they flee, or at best, curiously skirt the shadowy edges while carefully remaining ensconced in darkness. They savor the darkness. It is their world and their sanctuary. It is in their nature.

People are the same. Some thrive in the light while others reside in fear and darkness. Some want the light and will gleefully flutter to it. Others will flee. And still others live in darkness, while erroneously believing they live in the light.

(*"He that saith he is in the light, and hateth his brother, is in darkness even until now."* – 1st John 2:9, KJV)

Always remember this lesson from Nature, because Nature *is* God, expressed. While it's Nature we can see, what we're really looking at is God.

There are times when being a light to others occurs with such ease and synchronicity it feels destined to be. It's as if we're unwittingly an actor in some divine play, delivering our lines on cue at the perfect moment to direct a lost wanderer. But at other times, regardless of how many times we try to lead through example, or help, or influence someone, they continually retreat into the darkness. This is an issue with them, not with you.

Some souls simply aren't ready to progress. There are lessons they must still learn "in the darkness" before they are able to emerge and stay in the light. The moth may flock to the porch light, but they retreat at sunrise. They must learn to deal with certain Fears before they can dismiss those Fears. So know when to help, and when to move on, while always allowing your light to shine.

Chapter 22 – A lesson from plants

Don't change your morality for the people around you, change the people around you with your morality.

Okay. Time for a lesson from Nature.

A couple of years back, some family members gave my wife and I a large houseplant. This plant, a Peace Lily, was about 3 feet across and 4 feet tall. It's huge; laden with big beautiful cascading leaves and set in a decorative 10-gallon pot. We loved it, because it was a great way to pull some of Nature's beauty right inside our house.

To enjoy the plant, we placed the Peace Lily in a corner of the living room where it would be regularly seen and not forgotten. And over the next few months, we watered and fed it (my wife gets most of that credit). And during this time, the plant seemed to flourish.

Then something changed. Many of the outside leaves began to mysteriously wither and brown and the whole plant looked crestfallen.

To help the plant, we tried changing the plant food we were using and began keeping a closer eye on the soil's moisture levels. We also checked it for disease, but despite finding nothing, the plant continued to wither.

At our wit's end, thinking the plant had become root-bound or the soil was imbalanced, we went to the local nursery and bought a larger pot and a big bag of quality potting soil. We then carried the plant outside, very carefully re-potted it, and lugged it back to the living room. While this helped, it didn't end the problem.

Then it dawned on us. We had received this plant at Christmas and since that time the seasons had changed, as had the angle of the sun. Despite it being sunnier and brighter outside, the corner where that plant sat was now darker. Feeling confident we had solved the problem, we moved the plant to the opposite corner of the room, and within two or three weeks, the plant was back to its former glory.

I'm guessing by now you're wondering what this story has to do with the last quote about morality. So here it is:

Your words and thoughts form your perceptions. Your perceptions form your beliefs. Your beliefs are the basis for your morality (we'll expand on this in a later chapter). And depending on the slant of these beliefs, they are the "light" and "darkness" that form your morality.

What a lot of us don't like thinking is, just like the amount of sunlight in a specific corner of a room, our morality is in constant flux. As we are exposed to new thoughts and beliefs while passing through life, our morality can subtly morph and change over the seasons of life. Morality is rarely something that changes quickly, but rather, it slowly changes over periods of time through repeated exposure and new ideas.

Let me provide some relatable examples.

As we discussed earlier, long ago, women were viewed as possessions. As Man's beliefs about this changed over time, so did his morality. Today, treating a woman as a possession, especially as a sex slave, is not only immoral it's also illegal.

Slavery is another example. Man's beliefs about "owning" slaves has changed, and what was once morally acceptable is now morally unacceptable.

The same-sex movement is another example that's unfolding virtually before our eyes within modern-day society. Judging by polls, many people who abhorred the idea of same-sex marriage a decade or two ago are slowly moderating and finding it more acceptable.

This is how morality works. It's a lot like the plant story. When someone is having continual struggles and the "brown leaves" caused by making poor decisions in their life, sometimes all it takes to brighten their lives is through getting more or less light. It's a matter of balance. It's a matter of getting plenty of "light"… but not too much light.

And yes, you can get "too much" light. Think about it. If a person were to spend 24/7 meditating, or serving others, they're not taking time to care for themselves.

When it comes to attaining "balance" in life, the plants and trees within Nature are expert teachers. Healthy life for them means obtaining a balance of food (nutrients from Earth), water, and sunlight. Too much or too little of any of these can upset that balance and cause the tree or plant problems.

Similar to this, we are each three-part beings made up of body, mind, and soul. The body is our "physical" and "earthly" third of the whole. It's our "soil", and it needs feeding and proper nutrition. The mind is our more "fluid" and "flowing" third of the whole. It's our "water", and it needs monitoring to ensure we don't "drown" in our thoughts or emotions, nor "dry up". Our soul is the airy, ethereal and spiritual third of the whole. It seeks as much "light" as it can stand, but it requires a balance of "food" and "water" to process that light.

As you can see, each part of the whole influences and affects the other parts. If we spend too much time worrying over some problem, the stress can harm our body and "dampen" our spirits. If we spend too much time indulging in gluttony, or sloth, or "boozing it up", it can dull our mind and cause us to neglect our spirit. And if we spend 24/7 in meditation, our bodies wither and we neglect others.

It's all about having balance.

The thing is, over the course of time, some people get so caught up in life they neglect caring for their body, mind, or soul. And as a result of that neglect, they lose balance.

When this happens, we can help them by encouraging them to seek nutrition and exercise for their body, or help them understand whatever Fear in life may be plaguing them. We can also provide them with fresh ideas as "food for thought" and share different ways (perspectives) of looking at issues. But more than anything, we can be a "light" to that person, and "serve" them through example. We can be a light. We can do our part. We can be a positive influence to "sinners at the table". But we must also recognize that all people have Free Will, and whether or not they process that light is ultimately up to them. While a rose may flourish in the "light", a fern thrives in shadows. For even the darkness needs beauty along the pathway to light.

Chapter 23 – A gift for you

xxvii

Forgiveness is not a gift you give someone else, forgiveness is a gift you give to yourself.

Many years ago, when I was 16, I lived at the outskirts of a small rural town in Ohio, and attended a high school that was about 6 miles away.

On many mornings during the drive to school, I'd come upon a senior who attended the same school. There he'd be, with his thumb stuck out, hitch-hiking. This senior, who I'll simply call "John", wasn't the friendliest guy around. He came from a very poor family, always seemed angry, didn't have a car, and had been banned from riding the bus due to starting a fight with another student. He was brash, loud, and abrasive, and hard to find likable. But partially due to having a soft heart, and partially due to fearing his wrath, when I'd see him hitch-hiking, I'd stop and offer a ride.

During that school year, I picked him up or drove him home dozens of times. And after that school year, John graduated, got a job, and finally bought a car.

And then it happened.

The next year, on one particularly cold and rainy winter day, I had plans to attend a party at a friend's house who lived about 4 miles away. Unfortunately, when I readied to leave the house, I discovered my second-hand clunker refused to start.

Since a number of young, eligible girls had RSVP'd to be at the party, I was determined to go. The weather outside was horrid, in the mid 30's with light rain and wind, but that didn't deter me. With images of those young eligible ladies playing in my head, I bundled up in my winter coat, gloves, scarf, and toboggan, and began the 4-mile trek.

For two miles I sloshed through the rain. And since I was traveling a small country road the traffic was very sparse. On the rare occasions a car passed by I threw out my thumb and prayed for the driver to stop. But apparently, in the fading light, no one wanted to stop and pick up some drenched, unknown traveler.

And then came my salvation.

As I looked down the road, I saw John's car coming. "Thank God!" I thought. I was drenched and cold and miserable and ready to be at the party. Throwing out my thumb, I stopped walking and waited for John to stop and pick me up…only to watch in shock as he blew by.

I immediately ran into the road and vigorously waved my hands, thinking that perhaps he hadn't seen me. But to my dismay, his taillights faded into the distance.

It goes without saying, I was furious. I grumbled to myself all the way to the party. While dancing with a few girls provided temporary amnesia, I was still angry even after a friend drove me home. I knew it wasn't really that important in the grand scheme of Life. It wasn't as earth-shattering as a major illness, or losing a job you depend on, but it still left me feeling hurt and shunned and filled with angst. I felt very used.

Because John worked and I was still in school, our paths rarely crossed. And in the months after that night, we occasionally passed on the road, driving in opposite directions. He waved, I didn't. I passed him again one day while I was driving through town, and he was walking up the sidewalk. He waved, I looked away and drove on.

Some two years later, at the county fair, I ran into him. He walked up to me, smiling, with his hand stuck out for a handshake, and instead of shaking it, I went off.

As soon as I began talking... growling might be a more appropriate description... John looked stunned. He went on to explain that he never remembered seeing me hitch-hiking. He said he did pass up strangers hitchhiking, but assured me that had he seen me and recognized me, he would have picked me up. He went on to say how indebted he felt to me for all the times I had given him a ride, and how I was "a nice guy" and it had inspired him to be a nicer person. He apologized repeatedly.

As I began thinking about it, I realized that I had been wearing a heavy coat, had a scarf wrapped around my neck and mouth, had the toboggan pulled down as close to my eyes as possible, and visibility in the rain probably didn't help. And with that, I released the guilt and anger I'd been dragging around needlessly for two years. I forgave John.

What we can take from this is simple. It's wiser to forgive, rather than carrying around anger or hurt from some past event. *Forgiveness is not a gift you give someone else, forgiveness is a gift you give to yourself.*

All too often, we carry around invisible burdens. We remember the kids in elementary school who picked on us or called us names. We remember the girl or boy we liked, who rejected us. We sometimes even wish we could go back in time, to a certain day or scene, and do something differently to produce a different outcome. We all have felt hurt, and all try to cope with it.

Shackle too many burdens to your feet, and your wings will not lift you.

What really bothered me about the situation with John was, I had apparently been a positive influence to him … a light … without even knowing it. And I had made a mockery of that by giving him "the cold shoulder" through not waving back.

So what I'd encourage you to do right now, is don't make the same mistake I did.

Don't needlessly lug around an emotional burden that serves no one. Free yourself. *Do it for you*, because you love you, and then use that example as a light for others.

Release yourself from your burdens. Give yourself the gift of forgiveness, because you deserve nothing less.

As a mention here, nearly all of us have someone in our lives – a parent, spouse, good friend, or sibling -- who always tries to be there to support us and encourage us when we face hardship. Opposite to this, each of us probably know at least one person who would love nothing more than to see us fail. The creatures of the darkness rarely like the creatures of light. So if you have that person who would love to see you fail, remember this:

When someone would mistreat, misinform, misuse, misguide, mishandle, mislead… or any other "mis"… to others, they're obviously *mis*sing something in their lives.

They're missing the light.

So when someone would love to see you fail, forgive them, and *draw upon that motivation to succeed.*

Be forgiving. Be "for-giving". Because the person you are really giving to is *you*.

Chapter 24 – Releasing Fear

xxviii

Fear and guilt are your enemies. If you let go of fear, fear lets go of you. If you release guilt, guilt will release you. How do you do that? By choosing to. It's that simple.

Okay. For this chapter, there's a quote I'd like to "re-call" from a previous chapter. We called it forth then, and we are "re-calling" it now. Do you remember the quote shown below?

"At the heart of all anger, all grudges, and all resentment, you'll always find a fear that hopes to stay anonymous."

This section goes hand-in-hand with that quote about Fear.

At any time, we can choose to release Fear or guilt. And doing so is really simple, we only need to identify what Fear is causing us pain or guilt, recognize it for what it is, and then choose to release it, knowing that releasing it allows us spiritual growth.

There are some Fears, of course, that have purpose and merit that we should not release. A couple of obvious examples might be not walking into traffic, or jumping off a cliff. Retaining these Fears *serve us*. They have purpose.

As a general rule, Fears of *physical harm* are beneficial, whereas Fears relating to the *ego* are detrimental. (Some "phobias" are understandably an exception).

My story about John might provide us with a good example. I was not harmed *physically* by him driving past me and not stopping to pick me up (aside from some minor discomfort from the cold and rain). What was most harmed was my pride and ego.

And as you can see from that story, carrying around the anger and hurt from that experience did not serve me. It was detrimental. It was a burden I didn't need to bear. Now imagine that I had never seen John again before moving from Ohio to Virginia, and over the past 30-plus years, this hurt was still hiding in the "dark" corners of my mind. What benefit would my anger toward John serve… especially considering he barely remembered the event and surely would have forgotten it?

Most of us have a similar hurt or some type of guilt that we're lugging around with us. Subconsciously, we realize there is no benefit in carrying this burden and we'd be better served to "let it go". But our pride and ego object, because our pride and ego like the idea of having others "owing us something" … especially emotional debts ("he owes me an apology!"). The ego loves having people "indebted" to us, because to the ego, that makes it larger and more important. It serves the ego.

What the ego does is create an aggrandized, rose-colored image of Who We Are. And just like Fear or gravity, the ego has *purpose*. The ego is the part of our mind that tells us: "I can do this" …"I'm that good" … "I can overcome"… "I can win". And without the ego, Life's day-to-day Fears would reduce many people to cowering and sniveling. Early man may not have even survived without the benefit of an ego. It's what gives us our competitive spirit, and propels us to move on.

But like Fear, like darkness and light, the ego must be held in balance. We have to know when the ego is serving our growth, and when it's not. Otherwise, we start *being* arrogant and *ego*tistical. We can become these things, and *being* them only benefits growth of the ego, not our souls.

The thing is, the ego never likes losing *any* ground, so when information from the outside world conflicts with or threatens the ego's self-image, the ego likes throwing up "pride" as a shield. It's sort of that *"nanny-nanny-boo-boo I-can't-hear-you"* moment for the ego. Pride and vanity are the ego's favorite weapons. It uses pride to defend, and vanity to self-assure.

Our choice in life is, do we allow the ego to control us, or do *we control the ego*? Do we let the ego decide what we are *being* (pious, arrogant, etc.), or do we decide what the ego should *be* (a tool for our growth).

Do we bow to Fear or guilt, or do we let them go?

Releasing Fear and guilt are much like forgiving. In fact, they're usually the exact same thing. It's usually either a case of forgiving ourselves (guilt), or forgiving someone else. That is, by forgiving them, we are releasing them from any "debt" the ego perceives they owe us.

Even if the offending party has never apologized, the choice of forgiveness is ours. It is a gift *we give to ourselves*. (Give and ye shall receive). We are freeing ourselves from a burden that serves no purpose for us to carry.

Forgiveness is one of the wisest thoughts you can have. And with forgiveness, you can simply choose to release your "ball-and-chain" and hurt and guilt and fear. You already hold the key in your hand, you only need to unlock the shackle. And you are not releasing the burden *from you*, you are releasing yourself *from it*. It no longer serves you.

Some people can "let something go" very easily. They make the choice, and it's done. Others, however, find the process of forgiving and releasing themselves from their burden a little more difficult. As you may remember, I like using a stone for this process, simply holding it in my hand and visualizing all of life's harm draining into the stone. A friend of mine has a different system of cleansing. She writes a note saying, *"I forgive John for X"*, or *"I forgive Mary for Y"*, then she ties this note to a helium-filled (bio-degradable) balloon and literally "releases" it.

And there is one other way to release any harm you've faced:

Never be afraid to cry. Sometimes, nothing can cleanse the heart more than a few wet tears.

The next time you cry, imagine every tear you release being some part of the hurt you feel. Let it go. Release all the stress and pain. Get it all out. Cleanse your heart and soul.

Chapter 25 – Freeing others

When you forgive, you free your soul. But when you say I'm sorry, you free two souls.

Okay, as we've covered, forgiveness is a gift you give yourself. When you give "the benefit of a doubt" and forgive, you receive the gift of freedom (from that burden).

Saying *"I'm sorry"* differs. You are not only freeing yourself from guilt, you are freeing someone you've wronged or harmed from carrying an unnecessary burden. You're saying: "I recognize and feel the pain that I, or someone, caused you." Saying you're sorry is an acknowledgment. And just like giving love, or joy, or happiness, when you free someone from hurt they carry, you, too are freed. Two simple words can free two souls.

The irony is, uttering those two simple words is often one of the hardest things we ever do. Like sung by Elton John, sometimes, *"Sorry Seems To Be The Hardest Word"*. Our ego and our pride both yell in our ears, justifying whatever harm we caused, or telling us why the other party deserved it. But when your ego or pride scream for one thing, and your soul whispers another, always listen to your soul.

And always remember this: *To make mistakes or be wrong is human. To admit those mistakes shows you have the ability to learn, and are growing wiser.*

At some point or another, all of us make mistakes. We're humans, and that's what we do. Our mistakes are sometimes hilarious, and other times devastating. They are not things that make us "imperfect", they are our "perfect imperfections" that make us Who We Are.

Mistakes are "miss-takes". We either overlooked or missed something, or took something wrong.

If you learn from every mistake, you never fail at anything.

Think about that.

So never be embarrassed by mistakes, rather, be thankful for them, because they always present an opportunity for personal growth.

Be quick to forgive.
Be willing to say "I'm sorry".
Be thankful for mistakes.

Be all of these things to help your light shine.

Chapter 26 – Lest ye be judged

When people talk about you behind your back, they're not just behind you, they're beneath you.

People talk behind our back all the time. Marketing agencies, advertisers, credit card promoters, politicians, and a host of others talk about us in an anonymous sense, as members of a certain demographic or target audience. Others -- good friends, family members, or loved ones -- talk about us when they're reminiscing, missing us, or are concerned for our happiness, safety, or well-being. And as we all know, some will talk about us in a harmful way, criticizing our clothing, weight, appearance, intelligence, telling lies, or in numerous other negative ways.

The question is not a matter of *if* people will talk behind your back, *but how*.

By default, people make judgments. It is part of human nature. It is a necessary part of our survival and evolution. Early Man survived by making judgments of whether climbing a tree was a safer escape from an angry cave bear versus swimming across a river. Making judgments is a part of Who We Are. We do it multiple times every day. We compare the ingredients in pet food to see which is more nutritious, we make judgments at work and home to determine methods or actions that are more efficacious, we make judgments about where we live, our choice of home, schools for our children, whether toilet paper should unroll from the front or the back, and even whether ketchup is preferable on a bologna sandwich, vs. mustard.

Making judgments is a part of life.

We all judge. It's a part of human beings, and a part of being human. Often, we judge without realizing or mentally acknowledging we're doing it. We meet someone and think: she's pretty, he's funny, she's well-read, he's friendly ... and so on, and so on.

Having said that, I'd like to return to something we touched on earlier:

People who judge others tell more about Who They Are, than Who They Judge.

The simple truth is, we all judge. We often don't like thinking we judge, because it elicits negative connotations of Who We Are. We like to think of ourselves as "non-judgmental", and, of course, that's desirable. But the important question isn't whether or not we judge, but how are we *being* when we judge.

("For in the same way you judge others, you will be judged, and with the measure you use, it will be measured to you. – Matthew 7:2 NIV)

Who are we choosing to *be* when we judge?

Are we being a loving and loyal friend, or are we being jealous and juvenile? Are we choosing to be caring, or critical? Are we coming from a place of Love, or from a point of Fear? Are we being a light, or simply more darkness?

Again, people who judge tell more about Who They Are, than Who They Judge.

This occurs through *being*.

A judgment is merely an opinion. It's a conclusion based on the knowledge available to someone when they make an assessment. It may be correct, or it may be completely off base. But how someone is *being* when they judge is more than just an opinion. It's a declaration of Who They Are.

This is another place where pride and ego enter the scene. People who are mean or harmful when they judge are driven by pride and ego. They often have a very low self-esteem, and believe that by dragging others down, they are lifting themselves up. They erroneously think that pointing out perceived flaws in others, they are lessoning their own perceived flaws.

But think about this:

Fears and worries originate in the mind. Love and joy originate from the soul.

When a person makes harmful judgments, they are acting from the fears and worries of their mind. They joke about someone's hair style, or the clothing they wear, or their weight, or other "Earthly" matters. They abide the screams of their pride and ego, over the whispers of their soul.

When someone talks bad about us, (and sooner or later someone will, it happens to all of us), we can either choose to react from the fears and worries of our mind, or we can tap our soul and choose to create.

The first step begins with forgiveness.

It begins by understanding that carrying an unnecessary weight with us through our lives will only encumber our journey of Life encountering Life. It begins by understanding that they are acting from fears and worries and Earthly concerns, rather than acting from the love in their soul. They are in the darkness, and cannot clearly see. They are trying to "drag you down" which means by default, *"they are not just behind you, they're beneath you"*. They have not evolved yet to live in the light, they are still a part of the darkness.

But there is hope for them. God never gives up.

The second step is remembering that we must be willing to dine with the "sinners at the table" if we hope to be a positive influence and share our light. So if you hear of someone who has talked about you behind your back, be kind to them. Be friendly to them. And if the subject comes up, be quick to tell them you have already forgiven them. If the opportunity arises, give them a hug to show your sincerity.

Always be quick to forgive or give "the benefit of a doubt", because it will grant you the gift of freedom (and often respect, too).

The third step comes through understanding that not all creatures are meant for the light. Our first step should be forgiveness. Our second step is offering friendship and the opportunity to be a positive influence, but if the moth flutters away from the light, understand they are simply not ready.

Fourth, remember this:

When you continually worry about what other people think of you, they own you.

How many times have we dressed a certain way, or worn our hair a certain way, or behaved in a certain manner to meet someone's expectations? When we do this, we are essentially handing over our freedom to that person. We are allowing them to control us and make our decisions. We're not living for us, we're living for them. So if you want to "dress for success" to meet with a client at work, by all means, do so. But do it because *you want to*, not because it's perceived as expected. Do it because it's part of Who You Are.

And if someone talks behind your back because of your hair style, or weight, or whatever it may be, forgive them and try to be a positive influence, and if they return to the darkness, understand that they are simply not ready to be part of the light. Your path is not a better path, it's simply a different path.

Last, understand this:

If others can't end your suffering, why believe they can end your happiness?

I know it sounds trite, but happiness is a choice. We can decide to be happy at any moment. The question then arises, if we believe others can't end our unhappiness, why believe they can end our happiness? It doesn't make sense if you think about it. If they could cause you unhappiness, couldn't you simply just choose to be happy again?

So when someone talks behind your back, forgive them and try to be a positive influence in their lives. Try to lead them from the darkness into the light. Be a light not just for yourself, but to also guide others. But never let them control you. Never dress or behave purely to meet their expectations. If they truly love you for Who You Are, they will want to give you the freedom to express yourself, and be all that you can be.

Chapter 27 – Be surrounded with light

xxxi

Always surround yourself with people who lift you up, rather than hold you down.

We must always be willing to venture into the darkness and share our light with the "sinners at the table". And we must also be willing to be a light to those who have wronged or harmed us. Many will reject the light, but with each person who embraces it, we bring more light into a dark world.

At times, this is easy. Each time you brighten your own light, more and more people notice it and are naturally attracted. But at other times, we can get discouraged or sidetracked by the every-day calls of life. This is why it's important to surround ourselves with a core of like-minded people who are there to help us up if we stumble. Share your light with the darkness, but also share your light with those who share their own light.

Change is inevitable. Every moment of every day we are changing. We are changing physically, emotionally, mentally, and spiritually. Our challenge is to make sure any change we undergo results in our own positive growth. We can do this alone, but it's much easier when we surround ourselves with people who strive to lift others up, rather than pulling others down. We need people around us who understand the value of love and laughter, joy and inspiration. We need friends we can trust to serve as sounding boards and keep us grounded.

Thanks to the platform of social media, I've been fortunate enough to forge friendships with a number of great authors such as Sherri Cortland, Garnet Schulhauser, Jim Wawro, and many others who have written books about their own spiritual journeys and ideas. I'd encourage you to add their books to your reading list.

I'd also encourage you to visit https://www.facebook.com/DonaldLHicksAuthor. There, we have an ongoing conversation, and an open discussion of ideas to improve Who We Are, and bring more light to the world. So please come and join the discussion. Share your thoughts and grab a slice of Life's pie. Always surround yourself with people who lift you up, rather than hold you down.

And remember this…

Chapter 28 – The presence of Truth

xxxii

Regardless of how far a person runs, a lie will eventually catch up to them.

Above all things, always seek to fill your inner circle with people who are honest and worthy of your trust. Share your light with all, be quick to give the benefit of a doubt, but save a sacred place in your life for those you know who are both like-minded, and *honest*.

People can have great riches, but without honesty, they never have true respect.
People can have abundant love, but without honesty, they never have real trust.
People can have many friends, but without honesty, they never have loyalty.
People can have sharp minds, but without honesty, they never have admiration.
People can have fame, but without honesty, they never have honor.

Without honesty, a person's light may flicker, but it will never truly shine.

Without honesty, people are left with only lies.

And true love cannot contain lies.

For a moment, I'd like to go back to our "bucket of pure water/toxic waste" analogy for Love. Here's a quick reminder:

As an example, imagine you have two 5-gallon buckets. In one bucket you have 2 gallons of the purest possible water (Love). In the other bucket, you have 2 gallons of toxic waste (Fear). If you dip 1 gallon of toxic waste (Fear) and pour it into the pure water (Love), what do you now have?

Answer: Two buckets of toxic waste.

As we covered then, pure and unconditional Love cannot contain any type of impurity. If you take a glass of the purest water, and add a single drop of toxic waste (Fear), you have something less than pure, unconditional Love. It may still be plenty safe to drink, and it may look and taste like "Love", but it's something *less*. And we usually intuitively pick up that "something's not quite right", just like a mother cat often knows which kitten is ill.

Love is honest *always*, in *all ways*.

Love holds absolutely no deception or duplicity. It allows us to stand naked before those who love us, it allows us to be free. The moment we try to conditionalize that Love, and add a drop of Fear, we taint it. We make it "less". We make it something *other* than Love.

Honesty and Love share a common trait because, to *be Love*, you must also *be honest*. In the same way that we cannot conditionalize Love, we cannot conditionalize honesty. Anything less than pure honesty is an oxymoron. Anything less than pure honesty is just a lie by another name.

There are understandably times in life where *being honest* and *being Love* can seem difficult, but they are always the correct action for your soul. Let me provide a couple of examples.

Imagine your boss hands you a stack of papers he or she wants copied, and as you make these copies, you notice your best friend's name is on a list of upcoming employee layoffs. Do you tell your friend or not? What if your boss told you the papers were confidential? Do you tell your friend and break your boss's trust, or do you remain silent and break your friend's trust?

Life is filled with decisions.

As another example, suppose you happen to run out for lunch and see your sister's boyfriend seated across the restaurant, dining with another woman. Do you confront him? Do you tell your sister? And what happens if you decide to keep silent, and your sister learns that he was having an affair, and also learns that you saw him with the other woman but said nothing? Or what happens if you tell your sister, and it turns out the boyfriend was having lunch with his own sister or a client?

It's been said that "the truth shall set you free", but there are also times when the truth can be a prison (such as the two above examples). And I might add that there are times when it's kinder to not simply blurt something out for the sake of being honest. Sometimes it's not what you say, but how and when you say it.

There are times in Life when the Truth is crystal clear to us (such as when we're reading a memo titled "Lay-offs scheduled for "X" date" and see our friend's name listed for lay-off"). But there are other times when discerning Truth is a more difficult task. (Is he having dinner with a lover, or is it a client or relative?) At times, Truth can seem like some indistinct, elusive, and impalpable term that's difficult for us to capture.

So how do we know Truth? How do we recognize it?

Truth, most succinctly defined is: *That Which Is So*.
Non-Truth, most succinctly defined is: *That Which Is Not So*.

But let's make it even simpler, and consider the truth or falsehood of the following statement:

"You are currently reading a book (or ebook)."

We know this statement is currently *That Which Is So*, and because it is so, it is currently true. If you were to close the book (and I hope you won't) and go do something else, the statement "You are currently reading a book" would be *That Which Is Not So*, and therefore false.

Truth can change in an instant.

This is a very simplistic definition, and it helps our mind discern what is True, and what is Not True, but there are times in Life when our mind doesn't have all the information needed to draw a conclusion, and this is when we must rely on our intuition, rather than our minds.

Truth has no emotion or intention. It has no agenda or plan. But Truth is a gift from above – God -- and it has a valid purpose. It guides us in our decisions. It speaks to us through souls and we receive and recognize it through our *intuition*.

Think of it this way:

Chapter 29 – Guided by the light

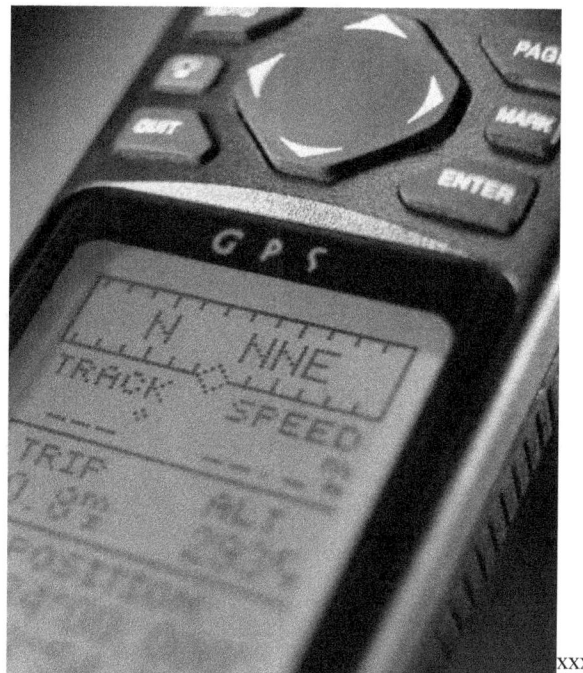

"Intuition is the GPS of Life."

How many times in life has someone told you something, but it simply doesn't rest well in your core? How many times has logic suggested you follow one course of action, but a hunch or your gut tells you to go in a different direction?

Our conscience and intuition are very closely related, but the information they act on comes from different sources. Your conscience is part of your mind, and it's a very important part, because it steers you to make decisions based on your morality.

Your conscience is your morality, expressed.

When you follow your conscience, you are expressing your moral beliefs (such as the value of honesty) to the world.

Let's delve a little deeper into this for a moment, for a fuller understanding. Our morality is formed by our beliefs of what actions are "right" or "wrong". If we believe stealing is a negative action, we find it "morally wrong". If we believe killing for sport as an undesirable action, we find it "morally wrong". If we believe "unselfishly giving" is a desirable action, we find it "morally correct". And when we, or someone we know "*gives, expecting nothing in return*", they are expressing their morality to us (and the world) through their actions.

Our conscience is an important part of us, because it lets us know if our actions are in agreement or disagreement with our morality.

Let me provide a more poignant example of morality based on beliefs:

Suppose a child is born in a third-world country where food is in short supply. Now suppose that in the village where this child is raised, if the villagers come across a feral cat or wild dog, they kill and cook that animal.

To those of us living in any modern society, the idea of killing and eating a cat or dog is morally reprehensible. We perceive (*perception is everything*) these animals as "family pets", and often view them more as "family", and less as "pets". Anyone who has ever killed a "family pet" by accidentally hitting it with the car, or starting the car on a cold morning and having a kitten clump against the fan (or any of countless other ways), knows how this can weigh on your conscience for weeks, or even years, after the incident.

But to this third-world child, killing a dog or cat is just as morally acceptable as killing a feral hog or chicken or cow, because the dog or cat is a potential food source, just like the feral hog. To this child, there is no moral wrong-doing.

If we hope to change the morality of this child, we must change the beliefs that create the child's morality.

Again, *don't change your morality for the people around you, change the people around you with your morality.*

Like many subjects, this requires walking a tightrope. It requires understanding that the person with "questionable" morality has reasons, and often very valid reasons, for believing what they believe. It requires introducing them to a different perception…. that perhaps that wild dog can be tamed and become not only an assistant in gathering food, but a loyal friend and companion.

To change morality, we must change the beliefs that create that morality.

Expressing your own morality through your behavior can certainly provide an example for others to follow, but changing someone's morality must ultimately start with changing their beliefs.

This is why "legislating morality" never works. When a person feels something is morally acceptable (or even "good"), and a law is passed forbidding that action or behavior, that law is perceived as silly or misguided. And when people don't take a law seriously, they will ignore it whenever possible. But through this, we can see another example. Speaking out against the law itself is futile. We can go on social media, and rant and rave over the pointlessness of certain legislation (and I've done it a few times), but until we change the beliefs of those who created and passed the law, we're banging our heads on the wall.

I might add here that sometimes, in the process of hearing the opposing reasons, our own morality may sometimes change. We must recognize that none of our paths are better than others; they are simply different. And through this, through maintaining an open mind, we hold open growth's door.

Chapter 30 – Sacred life

xxxiv

Until you are conscious of your conscience, you are morally unconscious.

Our conscience will guide us by reminding us of our morality, and our conscience is certainly an important part of Who We Are. But when it comes to conscience versus intuition, always side with intuition.

This is because our conscience works on an "earthly" level, whereas intuition is a gift and guidance from above. And there are cases where "we've gotten something wrong" and our morality is incorrect, and sometimes God, or our soul (or spirit guides if you like) must step in and try to change the beliefs that led us to that morality. None of us like admitting it, none of us like thinking it, but sometimes we're the ones "killing and eating dog". Sometimes our life experiences have led us to draw an incorrect conclusion that impedes our own growth. It's one of our "perfect imperfections". And this sometimes happens so we can learn a specific lesson during our stint here on Earth.

As any other author knows, any type of public writing is a mixed blessing. On one hand, it's incredibly satisfying to see the toil of your labor finally reach print. It's also very rewarding and gratifying to know that you might bring a smile to someone's face, or you might help someone you don't know (and might never have the benefit of meeting), who is struggling with some type of vexing and troubling issue. On the other hand, public writing leaves the author feeling very *vulnerable*. You know that there will undoubtedly be people who will criticize your wording, phrasing, ideas, intentions, and even Who You Are as a person. You will be called a hero by some, and a heretic by others. Your work will see acclaim from some, and acrimony from others. And there are certainly those who will both delight and deride the following story (and all parts of this work), but rather than run from that vulnerability, I simply choose to embrace it

So I remind all:

My path is not a better path, it is simply a different path.

I have made my own share of mistakes, and have a full list of my own "perfect imperfections". One of those relates to the issue of "killing and eating dogs" and a change in my own beliefs and morality.

Many years ago, during my late childhood, I was introduced to the sport of hunting through a couple of relatives, a couple of neighbors, and several like-minded friends I had. And from the time I was 9 or 10, up through my mid 40's, I loved to hunt. I loved many things about hunting… the sport of it, the "macho-ness" it granted me, the social interaction it provided, and probably most of all, the time it allowed me to be out amid nature. To me, being in and around nature was a wondrous event (and still is): smelling the mish-mashed potpourri of wild honeysuckle, acorns, musky rotting wood, and enjoying the beautiful artwork only Nature can provide.

I fell so deeply in love with hunting, that by my late 30's I quit a good paying corporate job and eventually took a low-paying position as a clerk at a small local sporting goods store.

While working there, I got to meet a variety of other sportsmen, and formed bonds with a few of the other hunters. When you work at a small sporting goods store long enough, you quickly learn (from the long-spun tales) which hunters are the trigger-happy "kill anything that moves" types, and which ones are more respectful hunters.

One particular year, I decided to hunt with a group of these more reserved, selective "still" hunters. We scheduled a deer hunt for a Saturday I was off work, and met at a friend's house in the wee hours before dawn, so we could be in the woods when the sun cracked over the horizon.

I was looking forward to getting a buck to fill the freezer, or a turkey for a warm winter meal.

While waiting for the stragglers to arrive, 4 or 5 of us began discussing current politics and the most pressing issues being debated. Somehow, we ended up on the topic of abortion, and I had a strange and disquieting feeling in my gut. Some of the other hunters called themselves "Pro-Life", and this in itself was a bit unsettling considering our purpose for gathering was to "kill-Life". To add to that, I was at odds with most of the group, because I considered myself "Pro-Choice". That is, I didn't believe abortion was desirable… I believed it was killing… but I didn't feel that I had the right to dictate someone else's decision. To me, that choice is between them and God, and I wanted no part of "legislating morality".

As the morning progressed, the stragglers showed up, and the hunt commenced.

About noon, I heard a shot fired from one of the guys not far from the tree stand where I was seated. Since it was time for lunch, I climbed down and clambered through the woods and brush to where he was. By the time I arrived, he had already started field dressing the deer, and as the entrails spilled on the ground, so came a tiny fetus.

For a moment I was shocked, and then I felt that deep unsettling feeling again within my core. Everyone there knew the local "rut" (the yearly deer mating season), occurred sometime in late October. And here we were on a January morning, a group of men --many of whom spoke out fiercely about the "iniquity" and "sin" of abortion -- yet hunting does they knew were pregnant.

I couldn't reconcile the two.

That morning in the tree stand… so many years ago… marked my last day of hunting with a gun. It changed my perspective, and my morality. From that point on, my hunting has occurred with a camera, and has never been more fulfilling. Because what I "shoot", is not harmed, and lives another day to be admired and "shot" again. From that day forward, I was still "Pro-Choice", but I became something truly closer to "Pro-Life" than anyone in that group, because:

If you believe Life is sacred, you must also believe unnecessary killing is sacrilege.

Just as a mention, I do not begrudge anyone who hunts for the purpose of obtaining food for their family. There is a clear difference between hunting for sport (and a trophy to hang on the wall), versus hunting for food. As fellow Nature lovers and animal advocates know, the living conditions for animals raised in hog, cattle, and chicken "factories" is appalling. Poultry are often raised their entire lives in overcrowded barns, cattle are prodded and sometimes moved about with forklifts, and breeding hogs are subjected to cages so small they can't even turn around. The treatment is inhumane. So if someone would rather take a deer or wild turkey that has enjoyed several years of relative freedom, to save a hog or chicken from being subjected to inhumane conditions, so be it.

My path is not a better path, it is simply a different path.

What I learned from that experience has since blessed me in ways I didn't expect. After swapping my rifle for a camera, I gained a new respect for Nature, and a renewed sense of the value of *all* Life in many ways. I realized that my true connection to hunting stemmed from my love of being out amid Nature. The camera enables this just as much as a gun. It taught me the value of "live and let live", and the benefit of being able to follow a deer or rabbit (etc.) through its natural life, which is incredibly rewarding.

It also taught me a new appreciation for vegans, and while I still haven't completely weaned myself from meat, I began gardening and there found a second love. In reality, I gained much more than I lost, which is what usually occurs when you follow your inner guidance.

Part 5: Nature

Chapter 31 – Nature, the teacher

xxxv

Nature will teach us many lessons if we take the time to visit her classroom.

Okay. You caught me. I know I used this "pearl of wisdom" much earlier in the book. And while I'm confessing my "sins", I admit it, it was me "Who Let the Dogs Out". I'm sorry, but I just couldn't stand to see them penned.

There we have it. I've "sinned". But this particular "pearl of wisdom" has so much depth and breadth it deserves more of our attention. If you think about it, Nature has taught Man an infinite number of lessons. At some early point in time, Man saw a stick or log floating in the water, and Man realized: "gee, if I attached some of these logs together, I would have a raft to float on". Then Man saw a vine spanning the trees, and suddenly conceived a way of connecting the logs. And then Man saw a bent leaf being blown across the water, and Man built a sail. And Man went on to build larger rafts, and larger sails, until he was able to travel great distances, thanks to the examples of Nature.

Nature has taught Man many, many lessons. From how to forage and build shelters, to turning Nature's resources into food, and drinks, and medicines, and ultimately all the things in modern day life.

Everything we currently have in our modern culture comes from Nature. Even "Man-made" synthetics ultimately begin as naturally occurring compounds. Nature gives us everything tangible in Life, and shares intangible lessons about love, perfection, light and darkness, racism, struggles, fortune and poverty, health, illness... the list goes on.

And Nature is not finished teaching. She never stops, because *Nature is God expressed*. All we need to do is visit Her classroom and silently observe and watch for Her lessons. Nature will gladly teach us about weakness and strength, hungry and gluttony, cold and warmth, darkness and light, kindness and cruelty, and hundreds of other lessons to those who will hear.

But there is a problem we must address as a society. In the eternal quest for profit and comfort, Mankind is rapidly destroying not just the classroom, but the entire school. As Joni Mitchell wrote (and perhaps prophesied) in *Big Yellow Taxi*:

"they paved paradise, and put up a parking lot... They took all the trees, and put 'em in a tree museum, and charged the people a dollar and a half just to see 'em".

As Garnet Schulhauser, author of *Dancing on a Stamp*, put it:

"We live on a beautiful planet that deserves our love and respect. Let us all do our part to stop the abuse of Mother Earth."

What Garnet said is very true. Nature deserves our love and respect, and that love and respect entails protecting and preserving her, and stopping the destruction of not just the classroom, but our entire planet. Nature still has many lessons to teach, and there are many lessons we still need to learn. The following is an excellent place to begin...

Chapter 32 – Nature, the giver

xxxvi

Have you noticed that everything in Nature, gives back to Nature?

Think about it.

Every part of Nature gives back to Nature. Nature endlessly gives through her own processes. She is the true "philanthropist of the year", every single year. Yet She is never named, nor ever seeks award or accolades. She quietly goes about her business of giving, because that's what Nature does. She gives without expectation. A bee flies from flower to flower, collecting the nectar offered by plants, and pollinates other plants in the process. The same plant that gives, also receives. Animals eat the fruit offered willingly, and then disseminate the seeds so new plants can grow in different areas.

Life gives, so Life can continue. Life serves Life.

If you take the time to watch Nature's intricacies, it's a beautiful symphony, with Life taking from Life and creating more Life, and simultaneously providing its own offerings to other Life, promising "more" for the future. It's an incredible and beautiful process. And through it, Nature teaches us a valuable lesson about the merit of sharing and giving.

These are lessons Man sorely needs to learn, because even in our concrete cities and wood and brick homes, we are still a part of Nature. Nature surrounds us. It is our habitat, and our own lives depend on Nature.

The problem is, all too often Man sees himself as "apart" from Nature instead of "a part" of Nature, and this illusion of separateness is ultimately destroying the very thing Man is a part of. Man is killing Nature with the intention of sustaining himself, when in reality, He is killing the exact Nature that sustains him.

That is an irony, but there is an even deeper irony. If you think about it, much of Mankind worships a God by one name or another, and simultaneously pillages and destroys the Nature that he calls "God's Creation", and then prays to that same God for help or deliverance when his plunder causes disaster. It's akin to intentionally killing someone's child, then begging the parents for release from persecution.

It would be very easy to judge and condemn those who do this. After all, to many of us who love Nature, the harm they cause makes us angry and causes us Fear. But judgment and condemnation is not the answer. Instead, we must strive to forgive them so we don't end up carrying a burden of anger, and we must try to change the beliefs that lead them to their behaviors. Calling names, or condemning their action only creates more darkness in the world. We must realize they still walk in the darkness. While they may believe they are awake, they are still spiritually asleep, and there is no benefit in trying to light a way for those who are sleeping.

Nature, though bruised and abused, is still happy to teach. If Mankind is to survive, the lesson we must learn is…

Chapter 33 – Nature, the provider

"When you nurture Nature, Nature nurtures you."

This goes hand-in-hand with an earlier "pearl of wisdom" we discussed: "If you nurture Life, Life will nurture you". And there is a very good reason the two are worded so similar, because Nature and Life are nearly synonymous. Nature is what sustains us, and without Nature, we cannot survive as a species. Life depends on Nature, and Nature depends on Life. Our entire planet is a part of Nature, and we must stop destroying our planet. We must understand that "preserving" is "serving in advance". It is "pre-serving". It is caring for Nature and serving Nature.

If we give to Nature, Nature will give back to us.

That's how it works.

Give joy, receive joy. Share love, feel love. Give to Nature… nurture Her, and She will nurture you.

But if we only take, and take, and rarely give back, we will ultimately deplete Nature. We cannot "pre-serve" a Nature that no longer exists… no more than we can preserve animals which are now extinct. We must serve Nature in advance. We must nurture Her, and She will nurture us.

And not just through food.

Nature can nurture us emotionally, mentally, and spiritually. She gives us food. She gives us the oxygen that we breathe. She gives us tranquility, is a teacher, and gives us glimpses of God, because Nature *is* God, expressed.

My love of gardening has taught me a valuable lesson:

Nature never rushes, yet everything gets done.

While this little "pearl of wisdom" can be applied to many facets of Life, (especially having patience), for our context here, we must understand that Nature completes Her tasks in Her own time, not ours. Her symphony is orchestrated by the weather and the four seasons, and ultimately God. In fact, as we'll later discuss in more depth, when we serve Nature we are serving God, because Nature is a part of God, and a part of God resides in Nature. I like to think of it as follows:

Chapter 34 – Nature, the artist

*Listen to the murmur of water and you'll hear Mother Nature.
Listen to the stillness beneath, and there you'll find God.*

Okay, time for another "confession". This may come as a shock to those of you who have read this far, but during the day, I work as a painter. That's my "day-job". My adult son and I co-own a small family-based painting and home-improvement company. We like being sober and dependable, and strive to do quality work. We paint mainly new construction homes, but also do "re-paints" of existing rooms and houses when our new-construction work is slow. The new construction work is tough, because the houses have no heating or cooling when we do the bulk of the painting. It can be very hot and dusty and dirty, or cold and clammy, depending on the season. The work itself is very dirty and strenuous to muscles and bones as old as mine. But like all things, it has its hardships and rewards.

While the new construction work usually pays better, re-painting rooms inside an existing home can be a pleasant respite. Not only are we blessed to meet a number of wonderful people, the aesthetic changes we make, and seeing smiles on our customer's faces can be a deeply satisfying experience. There's nothing quite like making someone feel like their home is fresh and clean and colorful. You can go home at night feeling you made a small difference in the world. And while it sounds trite, that feeling of satisfaction is the path to contentment. It has greater value than money.

At home, my wife and I are blessed by having a small, but warm and cozy, home situated on 25 acres. We have around 20 acres of hardwoods, with a small stream at the back of the property, and around 5 acres of open yard and space for our garden. My goal is to one-day retire, do more writing, and have our land designated as a Nature preserve so the local wildlife has refuge from hunting on neighboring parcels of land. That's the eventual goal. Until that time, I write on the weekends… especially in cold weather when our painting work slows… and spend most spring, summer and fall weekends tending the yard and nurturing my garden, while my wife nurtures several flower beds of her own.

I'm mentioning all of this for a simple reason. When my son and I and our employees repaint an existing home, we do the highest quality that time and the budget will feasibly allow. Yet even when we pour our heart and soul into beautifying a home, it never compares to the beauty God creates in Nature every day.

Nature isn't just filled with artwork, it teems with masterpieces.

I can't tell you how many times I've walked out the front door, stopped to "smell the roses" and admire the flowers in my wife's flower beds, and simply have been floored by the beauty and exquisiteness of a foxglove (see next picture), or stargazer lily, or even a simple marigold.

And as you take more time to appreciate and love Nature, a change occurs deep within you. Again, *"If you Love all Life you observe, you will observe that all Life will Love."*

We know from our dogs and cats and other family "pets" that animals have a capacity for love. Dogs, especially, love their owners… often even when that owner is abusive or neglectful. And because we know animals can love, we also know they can *feel*. In the case of dogs, we can often see expressions on their faces. We may occasionally misinterpret these expressions, but we know they feel. And when you begin to "Love all Life you observe", and watch the squirrels frolic in the trees, or deer graze in the field, you become more and more aware that they both love, and feel. *The more you love wildlife, the more wildlife you love.*

But there is a secondary point I'd like to share, here. Look beneath Nature's beauty and clamor and there you'll find God. God is constantly working "behind the scenes" with Nature, and the more you look for Him, the more you will find Him. Because....

Chapter 35 – Nature, as God expressed

When you can see God in small things, you'll see God in all things.

Throughout history, many people have asked: "If God exists, where is God?"

Perhaps the more appropriate question is: Where *isn't* He?

First, I'd like to say I don't begrudge anyone of having their own idea and concept of God. When people go through a search for The Creator, and establish a relationship with Him that comes from love and innocence and purity, it's a beautiful event for both them and the world. It's the addition of one more light to the darkness. And their ability to comfortably connect with God – whether that's through prayer, or yoga, or meditation, or intuition, or many other ways -- is ultimately more important than their idea of Who or What God Is. Why? Because once they've connected, He will teach them Who and What He is.

The problem we currently face in the world is that many people try to *use* God. They create a doctrine or dogma custom designed to fulfill their own selfish desires and to produce a specific outcome. They do not come from a point of purity or innocence, but rather, seek to deceive and empower themselves. They use "God" as a means of attaining power, or acquiring wealth, or fame, or even hope to dominate the world. Their "love" for God isn't love at all, because it is not perfect and unconditional Love. It is something less than pure. It's tainted with selfishness and is based deeply in their own fears. Hamas, the Islamic State, the Taliban, the Anabaptists, and countless other radical groups are suitable examples. Even a few greedy televangelists would fit the bill. They have a personal agenda they hope to fulfill.

At this point, I probably don't need to remind anyone about my path. But I'm about to do it again, just once more, so please indulge me.

"My path is not a better path, it is simply a different path."

I know I'm repeating myself a bit here, but for the sake of clarity, let me reiterate that I don't begrudge anyone of having their own concept or beliefs about God. Whether they believe in God, or Allah, or Yahweh, or The Source, or The Goddess, or simply The Creator is all irrelevant as long as they have forged that connection from a point of Love and Purity. The problem is, many people don't search for God from a place of innocence and Love. They search for a God who they believe will give them material wealth and comfort, or heal them in sickness, or assure their salvation. Putting it simply, they search for the God who best serves them (instead of the reverse).

Because of this, I believe it's actually preferable that people begin a relationship with God having *no pre-conceived notions* of Who or What God is. After all, anyone who's read parts of the Quran or Old Testament probably hold an image of a God who is angry and vengeful, unleashing blights and famines and destroying entire cities. The thing is, it's hard to open yourself and form a relationship to a God who induces fear. So please, if you're just starting a new relationship with God, or renewing your existing relationship, try to throw out any preconceptions and let God show you and teach you Who God Is.

Later in this book, we'll look at "Finding God". Since we're growing nearer to that point, I'd like to provide a summary of Who God is *to me*. I'm only providing a summary, because my concept of "Who or What God Is" isn't the focus of this narrative. Instead, the goal is to show ways that everyone can connect with God and discover "Who and What God Is" to them.

I would add that not everyone will share my beliefs… and that's okay… it's actually *good* because God is too big to fit into one mindset. God is larger than that. The more you learn about Him, the more there is to learn. It's not about having all the answers, but rather, knowing there are more questions.

Again:
Life isn't about finding the answers, life is about knowing there are always more questions.

So what do I believe about God? First and foremost, that He is my source, my creator, my parent, my friend, and a trusted confidant. God is Love and Life, and Love and Life are God. There is no separation of these two.

For me, God is truly "everything" and "every thing", because He is the energy that creates and forms *all* things. Our science teaches us that everything we can perceive with our bodily senses is formed from energy. "Matter"… the book you're holding, or the chair you're sitting in, are ultimately "energy at rest". Sounds and smells are energy flowing in waves. Everything we can touch and see, and even the things we can't touch and see (i.e. oxygen) are forms of energy. Moreover, science also teaches us that energy cannot be destroyed or created. It is eternal… constantly changing form. We are truly created "in God's image" because we are made *from* energy that *is* God.

I once silently observed a religious debate occurring between an atheist and a Christian apologist. The atheist proposed a question:

"If God is all powerful, can God create a rock so large that even He can't lift it?"

Obviously, if God can't create that size rock then He isn't truly "all powerful"… and if He can produce it but can't lift it, He's also not truly "all-powerful".

The Christian apologist discounted the question and went on to other subjects, and that was a smart move, because the question was silly and pointless. But when you stop to think about it, what if God *is* the rock that He creates, because that rock is created from Himself? What if the rock isn't "separate" from God, but is a part of God?

When you see God as the energy that forms all things, God is not only "all-powerful", God is "omnipresent". This also makes God "all-knowing" because if God creates a new life-form on Mars or in the jungles of Peru, God *is* that life form, and knows everything that life-form (or you, or anyone) experiences because each is a part of God. The micro is part of the macro. The smaller is part of the larger. The water drop is part of the ocean.

"For the body is not one member, but many. If the foot shall say, because I am not the hand, I am not of the body; is it therefore not of the body? And if the ear shall say, because I am not the eye, I am not of the body; is it therefore not of the body? If the whole body were an eye, where were the hearing? If the whole were hearing, where were the smelling? But now hath God set the members every one of them in the body, as it hath pleased him." -- 1st Corinthians, 14-18, KJV

When we look at the world, we see this pattern repeated in everything. If you look into an atom, we see neutrons and protons and electrons which look very similar to our solar system. Galaxies are a larger version of this, and universes are an even larger and more complex version.

Our body shares similarities too. Cells of like form are clustered together to form organs such as our kidneys and livers. These tiny cells ultimately form our body.

And again, we see similarities in Nature, where several different life-forms live in symbiosis in their own tiny eco-system. These micro-ecosystems are each parts of larger eco-systems, and eventually they shape Nature and Life. They each have God's signature, and each share their own beauty. And like the feet, and the eyes, and the ears, each thing has a unique purpose. We are truly "made in God's image" through having many parts, with different purposes, that create the Whole.

The more we look for God, the more we can find Him.

When you can see God in small things, you'll see God in all things.

Chapter 36 – Nature, as God's chapel

If the tree doesn't hug you back, it's not a problem with the tree, it's a problem with your heart.

I love trees. I've loved them since my early childhood. Some of my fondest memories occurred either in them, or around them.

When I was very young, around age 6 or 7, myself and the girl who later became my wife industriously built a make-shift treehouse in one of the maple trees in my back yard. I spent many hours of my childhood in that treehouse, both alone, and with friends. When I was troubled, or having some discord with my grandmother or kids from school, that tree was my refuge.

I also remember climbing the trees at a neighbor's house. Many of the neighborhood kids would gather there, and we'd compete to see who could climb the highest, or we'd simply sit in the branches and talk.

Over the years, I've learned a number of lessons from trees. Being a part of Nature, they will gladly teach if you're willing to observe and listen. My grandmother used to say that trees teach us to flourish where we're planted. That is true, but trees will teach us much more. Trees teach us about authenticity, hardship, getting along with neighbors, serving others, and lessons that are both large and small. It's all about your heart, and a willingness to observe and learn. One of my favorite lessons from trees is the value of being "Who You Are". A pear tree produces pears, and blossoms and grows in the way pear trees grow. It does not try to produce apples or peaches, or wear the bright blossoms of a cherry tree. Trees never put on airs. They are proud to be Who They Are.

Another lesson trees teach us is that the ripest fruit is always near the top, and sometimes rather than standing on the ground and picking "the low-hanging fruit", a little effort can produce sweeter rewards.

Trees also teach many lessons about hardship. If the limbs of a tree encounter some type of impermeable structure, such as the side of a cliff or a building, they will grow around it rather than trying to grow through it. And when the heavy winds or storms of life come blowing through, they teach us to bend, rather than being inflexible and breaking.

Another lesson trees teach us is our advantage over them. If the winds succeed in knocking over a tree, it can't stand back up. *But we can.* We have that advantage. So the next time we fall or get "knocked down", think of the tree and be thankful we can stand back up and continue on.

Trees also teach many lessons about sharing. Trees don't claim a certain acreage or ring of space, and fight off invaders: they share their space. Trees will often have the branches of their neighbors growing between their own branches, and theirs between their neighbors, and this process strengthens them against life's storms.

And trees also share in many other ways. They offer their fruits, and in turn, insure their future propagation. They provide sanctuary and nesting spots to birds and squirrels (each who teach their own lessons), and provide cool shady patches for picnics or rest.

Trees teach us all of these things, and much more.

Again, *Nature will teach us many lessons if we take the time to visit her classroom.*

We'll return to this in a moment…. But first, please indulge me in a brief detour.

For the first 19 years of my life, my grandmother (who primarily raised me and is loved and respected by a great number, including myself) insisted that I attend the small local church in the rural south-western Ohio town where I grew up. During my very early childhood years, I enjoyed going to church. Learning the Bible stories of Noah and Moses and Jesus and others was fun. And the activities during Vacation Bible School and Christmas plays and Halloween parties and other events were also enjoyable. But at age 9, this changed. At that time, while standing at the front door of our home, waiting for a thunderstorm to pass so I could go out and play in the mud-puddles, I was struck by lightning and had what's commonly called a "near-death-experience". That experience is a book in itself, and someday (if my guides lead me there), I may write of it. But for now, let me just say it changed my perspective of life, and the church's teachings. At my mom and grandmother's urging, I continued going to church, and tried my best to enjoy it. But church was never the same.

By the time I was 16 or 17, I was looking forward to the day when I was able to move out and would no longer be forced to attend church. It was a strange time for me, because being spiritual and seeking God was important, but what I felt and believed about God and Life were largely in contrast to the church's doctrine.

Because of my love of music, I joined a contemporary Christian rock band being formed by some friends. This was perfect at that time, because it appeased my Mom and Grandmother's desire for me to be active with the church, while it also allowed me to do something I enjoyed. For the next two or three years, the band and I traveled regionally, playing at churches of many different denominations and followings.

Prior to this, it had been "taboo" for me to visit other churches and hear their doctrines. But because of the band, I gained exposure to many different teachings. But like my own church, I quickly learned the doctrines of other churches usually weren't all that different, and almost all of them claimed to be the "right" (and often "only") true path to salvation.

Shortly after the band "disbanded", I moved out of my childhood home, stopped attending church, and my wife and I started our lives together. For a number of years, I was in a place of spiritual "limbo". I wasn't an atheist or agnostic, but was so involved in the day-to-day chaos of balancing work with raising children, attending their school events, repairing the cars and the home, I didn't make much room in my life for spirituality. I often missed it. And this is where we return to the subject of hunting. When I'd go hunting and sit at the base of a tree amid

God's creation, I felt truly at home. I felt spiritual and open. What I had learned was:

No church or synagogue pew can produce a higher awareness of God than sitting at the base of a tree and observing His creation.

Near the same time that I traded my gun for a camera, our children "flew the coup" and I began a quest of reading and studying everything I could find regarding religion and spirituality. Not being forced to adopt one of Man's teachings, I was free to explore spirituality without any *pre-conceived notions*. And I'm still on that journey today because, with every question and answer, *there is a new question*. And when that question is answered, there is another question. The questions are the essence of life, not the answers.

The picture of the beech tree (shown at the beginning of this section) is one of my favorite places to sit in our small woods. When I want to learn from Nature and escape from life's stress, or when am feeling spiritual and want to meditate, I often sit at the base of this tree (or another that's near a small babbling stream).

The thing about meditating under a tree is, sometimes when you first sit down, you'll sink right in to a comfortable position. But other times, bark or rocks or roots poke here and there. Yet as you relax and watch the squirrels or birds or whatever part of Nature it may be, all the aches and pains fades away. And soon, the tree becomes part of you, and you are part of it. You are hugging the tree, and the tree is hugging you back. And at that point, you know your heart is in the right place, because your heart and spirit and Life are One.

Chapter 37 – Nature's priests

Those who teach the most about humanity, aren't always human.

Plant an acorn and in sixty years you'll have a towering oak.

If you stop and think about that, it's simply amazing. It's a flickering glimpse into the magnificence of Nature and God. An acorn, something smaller than a golf ball, contains all the data it needs to transform itself into a mighty tree. It contains all the information necessary to grow roots and sink them into the ground, and have them extract minerals and moisture from the soil. It knows how to grow a trunk, to spread limbs from that trunk, and grow branches that reach for the sun. It sprouts leaves, which are shed each year, only to return the following spring. And moreover, the tree knows how to produce oxygen, and how to produce thousands of new acorns exactly like that which it grew from. When you stop and think about this, it's truly miraculous. It's astonishing. It's wonderfully remarkable. In a sense, it's the truest "Word of God", because it is God's instruction for life, encoded into Life.

And this is true, because you are like that tiny acorn. Encoded inside of you are all answers you'll ever need in life. It's already there. You already have answers to questions you've never thought to ask. It's akin to a yearling fruit tree that hasn't yet produced fruit. When the time is right to produce the fruit, the information will present itself. Everything you need to know to get through life is already inside of you, you merely need to know how to find those answers.

It goes without saying, that many people often have difficulty understanding this idea. And I am certainly not the first person to mention or introduce this principle. Much to the contrary, it has been explained and taught countless times, by countless others. And during these teachings, *many have listened, but did not hear. Many have looked, but did not see.* But be assured that everything a person will ever need for life is already a part of them. It's already encoded inside them.

I know for a moment it's going to feel like we're drifting away from our topic (Nature). But this is merely a curve in the path. We are still on Nature's path, even though it might feel like we're turning away from it. Soon enough it will be clear.

Whenever you have some vexing question, you already have the answer. The answer lies inside of you, you just need to find it. And to find it "within", you must look within. You must turn to your "in-tuition". You must turn to your own "inner learning".

If you think about the basic blueprint of Christian prayer, when someone is facing some troubling issue in life, they are instructed to pray and ask God for an answer. And what did God say regarding prayer?

"And it shall come to pass, that before they call, I will answer; and while they are yet speaking, I will hear." -- Isaiah 65:24, KJV

Think about that. *Before* they call, I will answer.

Before you have even thought to ask, God has already answered. Before you have even encountered some issue, and "call" upon God, God has already planted the answer inside you.

But again, *many have listened, but did not hear. Many have looked, but did not see.*

Let's look at one other angle, to help with this: "instincts".

When a sea turtle is born and emerges from the sand, it instinctively begins crawling toward the sea. The mother need not be present to "teach" or lead the young turtle. It operates on information already encoded inside it. It instinctively and intuitively knows what to do, and trusts its instincts.

When a chick (inside a chicken egg) finishes forming, it instinctively begins pecking at the shell. And after enough pecking and clawing, the egg is broken and the chick can emerge. The chick does not need teaching or knowledge of how to escape the egg, it simply trusts its instincts. It acts on information that isn't learned from outside sources... outside the shell... but already exists inside of it.

How beautiful and inspiring is that?

Acting on instinct alone, animals can accomplish amazing feats. They can build intricate nests and homes, know how to avoid (unlearned) hazards, know how to find food, interact with peers, form social hierarchies, and procreate.

And anyone who has seen a cat or dog give birth to its very first litter have seen these instincts in action. Without the benefit of Lamaze or nursing classes, animals instinctively know how to give birth, clean their newborns, and nurse and care for their newborns. And in some ways, they even trump humans. If one of their litter is unhealthy, they can sense it. It gives new meaning to getting a "cat scan". Without any type of medical knowledge or training or any veterinary exam, the mother knows which litter members are healthy, and which need more care.

It's a fascinating process and event.

And it grows from there, because where the instincts end, maternal love begins. When you watch animals interacting with their young, you can see their love and protectiveness. And you can witness acts proving how selfless mothers can be.

My family and I were once blessed to see one such act. Many years ago, we had three outdoor dogs who lived in a large wooded one-acre pen behind our house. Much to our chagrin, late one fall, the two females (a Golden retriever and a Labrador retriever) both became pregnant. Looking at their gestation times, our vet advised us the pups would probably come near the same date in February, and sure enough, come February, here they came. The problem was, being mid-winter, nightly temperatures commonly fell to the teens or twenties. While all three of our dogs had their own cedar-shaving lined dog houses, we simply couldn't bear the thought of puppies being born at night, when it might be 10 or 15 degrees. (Yes, we're softies). With no barn or other shelter available, my wife and I traveled to many local stores, seeking two of the 4-foot round plastic "kiddie pools" (and wow, these are tough to find in the winter... especially in rural areas!). Finally finding two pools, and buying a couple of bags of cedar shavings, we set up one pool in the office, and another in our bedroom across the hall.

Within a couple of nights, our Labrador retriever gave birth to 13 (yes, wow) puppies in the pool in the office. The following day, our golden retriever gave birth to her own litter of 6 puppies in the pool in our master bedroom. It goes without saying this was a busy time for us. We both had full-time jobs, one teenager still at home, and suddenly went from 0 indoor pets, to 21! Most of the time, chaos gleefully reigned.

At first, we were worried that the two mothers might fight, since they were both protecting their young and the rooms were very close. The two mothers could easily hear and smell each other. And with the kiddie pools being fairly shallow… about a foot deep… the moms could easily step out and venture out or into the other room. So to avoid any chance of a fight, we tried to keep the doors closed to each room.

And then something happened.

Somehow, someway, the doors got left open, and we came in to find the Golden Retriever in the Labrador's pool, helping the strained mother of 13 nurse her puppies.

From that point forward, we cautiously left both doors open, and quickly learned that we might find a black dog in our bedroom nursing gold puppies, or we might find a gold dog in the office nursing black puppies. Or both, in either pool. It was akin to one of the touching stories you might find on Facebook or other social media sites, and despite the anxiety of having 19 puppies to find homes for, we were lucky enough to live it.

Rather than fighting or competing, the two mothers worked in complete cooperation with the shared goal of ensuring both litters were safe and healthy. There was no bigotry or racism or self-serving intentions, only maternal and unconditional love.

At times, those who teach us the most about humanity, aren't always human.

Chapter 38 – Nature's masters

We may have pets, but when it comes to unconditional love, they are the masters.

Part One of this book covered the topic of Love. In it, I shared "My Three Rules" and we looked at unconditional love. Without recounting every aspect of love we looked at, there are a few tenets worth including here. We talked about the value of trying to "appreciate and love everything you encounter", and how "giving love (or joy) were the easiest ways to feel love (and joy)". We also looked at how "Love is the language that transcends all others", and how "the more we love all Life we observe, the more we will observe that all Life loves".

I mention these here, because all of these aspects of love were visible in the previous story about our two birthing dogs.

But Love is much larger than the very few lessons we've covered. *Love is giving*, and Love always has more to offer, regardless of how much we study and learn.

When you look at everyday life, there's a certain irony we can see. If you think about it, many people spend a lifetime searching for love or joy, *when they already have an endless supply right inside of them*. If they want to find it, all they have to do is give it.

Endless? Yes, indeed. This is another misconception much of humanity shares. Many people think they can only love a certain number of people, so they try to "conserve" their love, when what they should really be doing is freely "serving" their love to others.

Think about it. Has there ever been a single moment in life when you've been "all out of love"? Have you ever been forced to stop loving great-grandpa, so you could start loving a newborn niece?

We all know the answer to that. It's silly. But the thing is, people walk around life with this misconception floating in the recesses of their mind. They erroneously fear that if they love too many people, they might "run out of love". And they reserve some of their love, so when they meet the "right person" they will still have love left to give.

They hold back.

But I'd like to return for a moment to something mentioned earlier:

Love is a gift from above.

God *is* Love, and whenever we act with Love, we are being "Godly". Because Love is what God does. And this is where our "family pets" come into the picture (I like to think of them as just "family").

Working as a painter for the last 14 years, I can't recall the number of days I've come home from work, tired and dirty and sweaty, often hungry, and sometimes even grumpy over something that occurred that day, and there, waiting in the (full-length glass storm door) is our Shih Tzu (Candy). It doesn't matter whether I've been gone 4 hours or 12 hours, when she sees my work van come down the drive she starts dancing at the door (often pushing aside the cat that otherwise picks at her). And regardless of how much I'm carrying in my arms when I walk in, she'll dance around my feet until I set down the stuff and snatch her up for some loving. Regardless of what kind of day I've had, and more importantly, *regardless of what kind of day she's had*, she's always there to greet me with hugs and a kiss on the cheek (often many). Even on days when I'm harried and push her aside, carrying in groceries or other things, she refuses to give up until she has shared and shown her love.

When it comes to forgiveness, when it comes to compassion, when it comes to playfulness and being humane and not just human, we can learn much from animals. And most of all, when it comes to teaching unconditional love, they are the true masters.

Now as you know, I have my own path. Some will not share all my beliefs… and that's good, because I encourage everyone to find their own path. I believe that animals have souls, just like us. And I believe this due to a myriad of evidence I see in Life (and saw in "death"). But I do not condemn anyone who disagrees.

To an extent, I once did condemn. Many years ago, when I still belonged to organized religion, a preacher and I were having a discussion about this subject, and he declared that biblically speaking, "animals have no souls". I disagreed with him for many reasons -- some biblical and some as evidenced in Life. For one, *the Bible* mentions the "soul of a turtledove" (Psalms 74:19) which is clear enough to me, but when you add in the latter verses of Ecclesiastes 3 (19-23), especially regarding "one breath", it becomes even clearer. And as the conversation went on, and turned more to a debate, it became increasingly evident to me that this preacher felt that all of Mankind was competing to be "God's favorites", and he didn't like the thought of animals being part of the competition (he saw). To me, it was an extremely small idea of what God, Heaven, and the Afterlife really are. And by the end of the discussion, I had more doubts as to whether he had a soul, than the animals I knew. I silently condemned him for it.

That was wrong of me.

I have grown much as a soul since then. My perceptions and morality have changed. I now understand that everyone must find their own path and what rings true inside them. Finding your *own truth* is of utmost importance. Whether our truths agree at any given moment is less important. What really matters is the outcome. The truths we each encounter along our paths, even if different, will ultimately lead us to the same destination of the journey.

Each truth we find leads us a step closer to God. (Even if we're following different paths).

As a visible example, think about this. At this exact moment, my fingers are typing and I am writing this book and trying to convey a message. The pages below this text are blank (aside from my ideas and God's inspirations). This is an undeniable truth to me.

But to you, there are many more lines and pages beyond this one. This is an undeniable truth to you. Yet while our truths are different (and relative to time), we will ultimately share the truths that (1) I wrote this book, and (2) you were gracious enough to read it (thank you, I hope you find it worthy of sharing). Those two truths will both be absolute for each of us. And hopefully, things that you have read this far (and will read on future pages) will also ring true to you, because the more truths we share, the closer our paths become. And any path is easier when we have someone helping us navigate the pitfalls and obstacles.

To me, when I look into the eyes of a horse, or Labrador, or cat, or rabbit, or whatever animal it may be, I see a soul. It is a truth along my path. If someone says, "I'm not sure if animals have souls" my answer is simple:

"Look into their eyes."

And if they say, "I still can't see a soul", my answer is even simpler:

"Look longer."

If you Love all Life you observe, you will observe that all Life will Love.

The more we love animals, the more we see they love. And just like us, they use that love to form relationships. They play. They feel pain. They face suffering and hardships. And if they can feel emotion, they are self-aware. And if they are self-aware, they have a soul.

We share a common union with animals, and that is Nature. Just as they are a part of Nature, so are we. If Man is to survive, we must recognize this "common union" and merge it into "communion". We must serve "communion" with Nature, which in turn is with God. For when we destroy Nature or needlessly take Life, we are destroying ourselves.

So remember….

Chapter 39 – Nature, Life, and God

Life is more than just a bump in the road. All life is sacred.

To me, *all* Life matters, and *all* Life is sacred. Because all Life is a part of Nature, and is ultimately a part of God.

Let's play a little game to help understand this. First, read the following paragraph:

Life IS. Life is that which surrounds us. Life is that which sustains us. Life is that which changes, and continues, and never dies. Life is a part of You, and You are a part of Life. You and Life are made from the same "stuff", the same energy, and that energy is the essence of Life.

Make sense?

Now re-read the paragraph, substituting the word "God" everywhere the word "Life" appears.

Still make sense?

Try again by substituting "Nature" for Life.

As you can see from this, God, Life and Nature are interchangeable terms, because

Life and Nature *are* God, *expressed*. They are an extension and part of God. And you, being an intricate part of Life and Nature, the eye or the ear, are also an extension and part of God.

For this reason, all life is sacred.

Because of my deep love of God and Nature, this is an issue I'm passionate about, and it may show in the next paragraph. In all honesty, it is challenging not to launch into a rant (smile). But while a rant may feel good during the moment, it seldom accomplishes anything, so I'll do my best to refrain, and please bear with me.

As we all know, there are members of our society who refer to themselves as being "Pro-Life". These members do support saving the lives of fetuses, and that is admirable. *I applaud them for that*, because supporting the sanctity of the unborn, those who have no voices, is preferable to not supporting any life at all. Unfortunately, with many of those I've met, fetuses are often the extent of their "Pro-Life" ideology. These same individuals, who proudly (or sanctimoniously) wear the title of "Pro-Life" are often the same ones who advocate destroying Nature in the quest for wealth or comfort.

I would ask you to consider this:

When someone places more value in saving money, than the value they place in saving Life, they have "misplaced" their values.

But it goes deeper. Often, these same "Pro-Lifers" favor the death penalty and support wars. There's a deep irony here if you think about it. For one, they often base this "Pro-Life" stance on a religion they describe as having a message of "love and redemption" (even as they advocate capital punishment and fight enemies). And secondly, the falling bombs in the war they advocate may kill pregnant women and many of the *fetuses* they so ardently otherwise defend.

For those of us who love Nature and value *all* Life, it can be frustrating. But rather than indulge in fear and anger, we must choose a higher path. We must strive to change the beliefs that lead to this mindset. We must help them understand the value of *all* life. As the term "Pro-Life" implies, we must support *all* Life.

Anything less is a misnomer.

Anything less is simply a lie.

Because again:

If you believe Life is sacred, you must also believe unnecessary killing is sacrilege.

On the other side of the equation, there are unfortunately times when killing is a "necessary evil". There are times when people are stricken by mental illness, or consumed by greed, or jealousy, or anger, or their own fears, that they are intent on destroying everything and everyone around them, even the innocent. And as a society, we must always protect the innocent. Going back to Rule #3, we must protect ourselves (and those we love) from harm. We must defend life, even if it requires taking life, but we must take life only when it is the last possible alternative.

We must learn that *when people devalue any one Life, they devalue all Life.*

Every caterpillar that dies is one less butterfly we can enjoy next spring.

Life and Nature are a part of Who We Are.

Part 6: Finding God

Chapter 40 – Losing your mind, finding God

To follow God, one must be a little "out of their mind" (and "into their Spirit").

.

My mother was a foster child. In an era when foster children were common, around the time of WWII, she was taken in by my "grandmother", who raised foster children, and subsequently raised my mother.

Around the time my mother was finishing high school, she and my father got married and moved into a very small home next door to my grandmother's house. Shortly thereafter, I was born.

When I was 3, my father left us. It goes without saying, this was a very troubling time for my mother. Due to the strain of that loss, combined with what was likely postpartum depression (a condition not understood during the 1960's), she fell into a deep despair and could not care for me. Because of this, I was eventually placed as a foster child with the logical choice, my "grandmother".

All of this resulted in a difficult-yet-wonderful childhood. On one hand, I was mercilessly teased and ridiculed as "the kid with no dad", a "bastard child", or "the kid with the crazy mom". And adding salt in the wound, both my grandmother and my mother were very poor, meaning I rarely had the latest clothes or toys or even two nickels to rub together (and another source for teasing). I have many, many memories of dragging a Red Ryder wagon up and down the rural roadside, searching the grassy ditches for soda bottles I could redeem at the local grocery for .02 cents each.

Yet all was not bad. I always felt loved by my grandmother and mother, and my grandmother was (and still is) a diligent and determined worker who could outwork many men half her age. She is also compassionate. Over the years, I saw her make countless sacrifices on the behalf of myself and others. She was a great example for me as I grew up, and remains so now.

I also had a few friends who either understood my plight, or shared similar hardships of their own… often both. Some of these friends didn't live in the neighborhood, but frequently visited relatives who lived there.

During the hot, redolent summers of my childhood, I often engaged in passionate games of kick-ball or tag with the neighborhood kids. At other times, we played hide-and-seek, tag, climbed trees, or rode bicycles, seeing who could perform the bravest stunt (which often resulted in scratched elbows or gravel embedded in knees). And despite the sometimes painful mishaps, those days were fun and replete with all the ingredients for fond memories.

When I wasn't playing with the local kids, or scavenging redeemable bottles, or seeking solace in my treehouse, I spent much of my time exploring along the banks of White Oak Creek. The creek was my favorite place in the world. There, Nature always awaited me, offering a plethora of mysteries and lessons to curious eyes. And there, along the muddy banks of the creek, my love of Nature was born.

At other times, especially on rainy days, I went with my grandmother to work. My grandmother worked as a housecleaner for a local doctor, dentist, and a few other affluent families in the area. This provided me the opportunity to play with other kids, or to watch large color TV's (as opposed to our tiny black-and-white model), play with newer toys, and learn about other amenities that money could buy.

On one particular such outing, when I was around age 5 or 6, the home where my grandmother was working had a stove that piqued my curiosity. In our own home, we had an ancient gas cooking stove which had to be lit each time it was used. But this new home had something called "an electric stove", with no need to strike a match and light the burners… you just turned a knob. And even more interesting, the burners had no flames. I found myself in disbelief that – with no fire – this fancy stove could even work. I was convinced that the owners had wasted their money on the contraption, and to test that theory, I touched one of those glowing burners.

As you can guess, I was burned. Not badly. Just a nice fat blister on one finger, but well enough for me to learn much from that experience. For one thing, I learned that fire (and the sun, and hot asphalt) weren't the only things that burned, and I would never intentionally touch a stove burner again. But more importantly, I learned that regardless of how many books one might read about "the pains and perils of burns", or how painful someone tells you burns feel, nothing compares to "first hand" experience.

This is true of God and our experience of God.

Throughout history, different cultures and people have formed very different beliefs of Who or What God is. To some, God was a spirit that lived in the forests or wilderness. To others, God was a Man who once walked the Earth. To others, there were many Gods who often battled amongst themselves. And to others, God is some despot who sits atop a golden throne, issuing punishments or blessings.

When you ask someone Who or What God is, the answer you receive depends on who you ask.

It's similar to Truth, as we spoke of it earlier. God can be different things for different people.

The word "Dogma" also comes to mind here.

"Dogma", spelled backwards, is "Am God". When a person allows someone else's dogma to become their God, they have things backwards.

Which brings us to our first point (of three).

If you want to know Who or What God is, you must ask You. You must look inside yourself to find that answer. Because, *before you have even thought to ask, God has already answered.* The answer is already there. You only need to find it. You only need to do some "soul searching".

Over the course of time, many religions and spiritual leaders have taught this lesson. They have taught that you are a temple, and the spirit of God dwells within you (1st Corinthians 3:16). This concept has been taught in Islam, Shinto, Rastafari, Buddhism, Hinduism, the Bahá'í faith, and countless others. *But many have listened, but did not hear. Many have looked, but did not see.* (Including many of the teachers). They continue to search for God in *outside* sources, rather than searching the most direct route possible: *within.*

When it comes to your own personal relationship with God, nothing trumps firsthand experience. No one else's opinion or belief can ever teach you as much about God as your own personal experience and relationship with God. A secondhand account never compares. No Scripture or book (no, not even this one) should ever serve as a substitute as your connection and journey with God. No account will do, because any second-hand account will ultimately be "no account" when compared to a personal relationship you can form directly with God. Books may be helpful. They may aide in the process. But they are only stones along your path. They are messages to lead you to a specific understanding, or help point you in the right general direction. They may be a part of "the way", but they are never *all* of "the way". The rest of "the way" is up to you.

It is this reason I've only included a "summary" of my idea of Who and What God Is. Because for the Truth to speak to you, you must find it inside.

The answers await inside you, waiting for you to find them.

If you will notice, many of the words Man has created to express himself inadvertently back up the principle of knowledge existing inside of us. *In*stincts is certainly one example. As are *in*tuition and *in*spiration. They all refer to knowledge or information coming from "inward" origins. They all begin inside us. Their source is "with*in*".

We touched on this subject earlier when we looked at "instincts", and looked at how "instincts" are information God has encoded inside of His creation. But let's expand on that, and now "pull in" *in*tuition, *in*spiration, and even *in*telligence.

If you think about it, when we observe what Man calls "lower" Life forms (single cell organisms, simple plants, reptiles, etc.) we see that these simpler life forms rely heavily on their instincts for basic survival. As we move up the animal chain and look at the "higher" Life forms, however, we begin to see Life forms which feel emotion and are able to gather data and learn from their environment. They essentially "pull *in*" information from outside sources to build *in*telligence.

In the case of these "higher" Life forms, they begin their lives by relying on *instincts* (i.e. – babies suckling, crying, crawling, etc.), but eventually develop emotions and intelligence and no longer rely solely (or "soully") on instincts. In a sense, they begin suppressing this internal information and relying on outside sources. They begin relying on themselves instead of God, much like a teen begins asserting their own independence from their parents. That is, until they face some "fight or flight" situation, and then their survival reverts to instinct (much like a child comes running to Mom or Dad when frightened or endangered). This is a part of the process of growth.

Which brings us to our second point:

For many years, religions have taught Man that he is not to rely upon his own reasoning or intelligence. One particular Bible verse that pastors or preachers frequently throw out to deter or admonish their congregation from relying on their own ideas is found in Proverbs. It reads:

5: "Trust in the LORD with all thine heart; and lean not unto thine own understanding." -- Proverbs 3:5 KJV

This message seems clear enough:

Trust God, not your mind.

It's really very simple.

Or is it?

If you think about it, this teaching (in this context) creates internal conflict, because the followers of many religions are taught that they are a temple, and the Spirit of God (especially the Holy Spirit) *resides within them* and is there to "teach them all things" (The Bible, John 14:26). Yet now, they are being told not to "lean unto thine own understanding". They are being told to submit all authority of spiritual matters to the clergy. Or to submit all authority to the *Bible* (which often translates to "the clergy's interpretation of the *Bible*"). The message is essentially: do not follow your own understanding (despite the Holy Spirit dwelling within you). And for people who have not directly connected these two different teachings, they have a vague and disconcerting feeling that "something is amiss" when they hear certain teachings of organized religion.

So is the message of this verse still simple?

Suppose it *is* simple in a different way, with a different interpretation. Suppose what this verse is really teaching is not to rely on your intelligence -- which is information you have pulled in from outside sources -- but rather, to truly "trust in the Lord" (the Holy Spirit)... *to override the mind and trust intuition.*

The "higher" animals (Mankind included) differ from the "lower" ones in two ways. For one, we have "higher" intelligence which provides us with a questioning mind and the ability to exercise Free Will and make choices and decisions. We are not forced to blindly follow instinct, and this ability is truly a gift (and can equally be a curse).

In addition to intelligence, we also have intuition, which is the next step up the growth chain. Much like a "medium" Life form can occasionally override it's instinct and operate by the mind, the "higher" Life forms can override intelligence and operate through intuition.

Again, as we discussed much earlier:

Life isn't about finding the answers, life is about knowing there are always more questions.

And when it comes to these questions:

The mind sees questions, and seeks answers from without.
The soul sees questions, and seeks answers within.

This brings us to our final point in this section.

When we observe Life (especially with Love), we can see a pattern. The "lower" life forms survive purely through instinct... internal instruction from God. "Higher" life forms... God's children... begin life by surviving on that same instinct, but as they develop both emotions and intelligence, they are no longer forced to follow that instinct. They can exert "Free Will" and override their instincts. They can decide to suppress their instincts, and this ability is what makes them "higher". It does not mean "better" (and there is a distinction). It simply means they are more evolved – much like an 8th grader is more evolved than a 1st

grader. They are a few steps ahead on their path.

The path to God involves becoming continually aware of our soul.

It is the next "higher" plateau.

As we each age and mature, we eventually learn that there are times in life when we must use our intelligence to override or suppress our emotions. This is an important tool when making decisions, and especially during moments of great duress or disaster. And this ability marks the next "higher" plateau on the pathway of development… the spiritual path leading us back to Home, and back to God. Because when a person can suppress their emotions and objectively understand what they are experiencing or undergoing, it gives them the chance to pause and examine if they are acting from a point of Love, or one of Fear.

It is a moment of stillness.

We quiet the emotions and ego to listen to the mind and our intelligence. (But the mind and intelligence are not our highest source… we'll come to that).

Let's look deeper at suppressing emotions and especially the ego, and "cognitive dissonance" might be a good place to start. For those who don't know, "cognitive dissonance" is the mental stress a person feels when they have one set of existing core beliefs, and new information or evidence presents itself which contradicts or disproves those core beliefs. As a very basic example, let's say that "Steve" owns a certain car, and he believes this car is worth $2000.00 (because five years ago he saw an identical model sell for $2000.00). Now let's assume that Steve decides to trade in "Ole Betsy", and when he goes to the car dealership, the dealer only offers him $500.00, and shows him the bluebook showing "Ole Betsy" is really only worth $300.00. The doubt and anguish Steve would feel -- the threat to his ego -- is called "cognitive dissonance".

But let's go further. Let's say that "Jane" is a member of "The Great Blue Elves Church", which was founded in 1701, and is based on a manuscript found in a cave in Scotland in 1659. And let's say that Jane not only has an emotional investment in her religion (she enjoys participating), she also has invested time and money into it (i.e. – time spent sitting in the pews, volunteering for Elf activities, and money given through her tithing, etc.). Now let's say that a second manuscript is discovered, and it was written by the same author as the original manuscript, and in it, the author admits the story of "The Great Blue Elves" was really just a fable.

What Jane would feel upon learning this new information is "cognitive dissonance".

The thing is, "cognitive dissonance" stems from Fear. For Jane, it would stem from many fears ... that her "non-Elf-believing" relatives or friends might laugh at her for being "suckered", that all her time and money were wasted in vain, and especially... that she will have to find and learn a whole new religion. Many people cannot move beyond this state. They will try to suppress information, ignore it (the nanny-nanny boo-boo I-can't-hear-you), or even lie to themselves because of these fears. They allow emotions and the ego to override intelligence. And as you can see, they cannot grow. They cannot progress. They are trapped in the cave of blackness.

But there is a flip side to this equation. Overriding one's emotion and ego with intelligence isn't always the "highest" decision. For example, if someone's child is being abducted by a knife-wielding thug, an unarmed parent might override their fears and act from Love and charge the thug, despite logic and reason.

What's most important is the reason. Is a decision made by Love, or from Fear?

As a general rule, if it comes from Love, follow the emotion. When it comes from Fear, override it with the intelligence (or with a different action that stems from Love).

But there is another "higher" plateau that awaits us.

When we learn to quiet not just our emotions, *but also our minds*, and listen to that "still small voice" we climb another step toward God.

Again, *to follow God, one must be a little "out of their mind", and "into their Spirit"*.

We learn that...

Chapter 41 – You are worthy

"In the stillness of life, we find our higher self. Be still and God is with you. Be still, and you are never alone."

If we want to find God, we must "quiet our minds" and trust in our spirit.

And this is the journey we are all on.

All of us.

Both the "lower" life forms who are behind us on the path, and the "higher" life forms.

Our goal… our journey… is to find God.

So how do we do this?

There are many ways to communicate with God. God did not set up just one exclusive method of contact. He does not restrict communication, nor require someone to pray in a certain way, or at certain times. Nor does God answer to only one specific name. If you prefer to call Him the Creator, Yahweh, Allah, the Great Spirit, the One, the I Am, Jesus, God -- whatever name you prefer -- He will answer. Even if you prefer "The Goddess", with the pronoun "Her", She will still answer ("Him" and "God" are simply my own preferences, despite knowing God has no specific gender). God always "accepts", and never "excepts". He is always there, always ready, in all ways.

It's akin to modern communication. God has (truly) wireless phone service, but He does not limit communication only to a call (prayer). God accepts text, email, social media, citizens band radio, and will even respond by Morse code if that's your preferred method of communication. How you connect is inconsequential. What's important is finding a method that fits your life and can be easily accessed.

Before we move on, there's an important subject we need to cover. As you may remember, in a previous section, one of the "in" words we were going to "pull *in*" was "inspiration".

It's now time to do that.

Putting it simply: *any inspiration is the recognition of God's hand at work.* It's the recognition of God speaking through someone. And it's not restricted to just inspirational quotes or ideas. When we see someone act with great sacrifice stemming from love or compassion, we subconsciously recognize God (Who is also Love) working through that person. On a soul level, we recognize the Divine *in their actions* and feel it, and want it in ours. It's a fleeting "re-union" of the soul and God. It's akin to being in a two-story mall, and catching a distant glimpse of a loved one just as they disappear into a store. We recognize them and feel a flutter of emotion that's nearly synonymous with "inspiration". And just like wanting to be with that loved one, when we recognize the Divine it also inspires us to want to *be* Divine. It inspires us to "step up to the plate" and act with the same kindness or sacrifice that we witnessed in the behavior of whoever inspired us.

This is what inspiration means. It's recognizing God at work in Life, and wanting to live *up* to that standard. It's a matter of seeing a glimpse of the Divine, recognizing it, and longing to return to the Divine and be with God. Inspiration is always about moving upward, not downward. It makes us want to live higher, not lower. It makes us want to live like God…. to not just feel Love, but *be* Love. We aspire to live inspired.

But here's where Fear usually shows its ugly face.

Many of us do not feel *worthy*.

While we may feel okay with talking *to* God… often pleading or bargaining… we don't feel worthy of having God use us or talk directly *to us*.

We tell ourselves, "we are not worthy."

And with that, we abandon Love and say hello to Fear.

The thing is, many people have a preconceived notion that God only inspires or communicates with certain people. For some, they believe that God inspired a few select "chosen ones" two-thousand years ago, and then completely stopped inspiring. Their idea is that God put forth His word, and is now sitting silently in Life's bleachers, watching as the game plays out, waiting to name the winners and losers, the cheaters and the heroes.

For other people, they believe that God still selectively inspires, but He reserves this inspiration for only people who have followed all His rules, for those who have lived chaste or pious lives, and through their behaviors have "gained God's favor" (i.e. –The Pope or upper clergy).

There was a time in my life, back in the mid 1990's, that I believed I was not worthy. At that time, I was at an exceptional low. I was at "rock bottom". I wasn't even sure I wanted to continue living. I had a good job, but I hated it. I had a nice home, and a newer car, and lots of nice "things", but felt trapped by the bills that accompany those things and the battle to "keep up with the Joneses". Our kids had just "flown the coop", and that left my wife and I both feeling a bit lost.

And then things got worse. I fell into such a depression ... the "pit of Fear" as I now call it... that I lost my job. At nearly the same time, my wife's company decided to downsize, and she lost her job. It was a very troubling time for us.

One particular day, when I was feeling exceptionally angry and fed up with life, and longed for that childhood treehouse where I could find solace, I drove to a local creek, and wandered along its banks, seeking solitude. I wanted a good cry. Again:

Sometimes, nothing can cleanse the heart like a few wet tears.

Having hurled a few skipping stones angrily at water, I finally plopped down, defeated, with a stone still in my hand, wishing with all my worth that I could send every bit of negativity in my life into that stone... then just fling away.

And that's when it happened.

As I was sitting there, tears streaming down my face, somewhere inside I heard a small voice simply say:

"Be still, and know that I am God".

Although that was the only message I heard that day, it began a spiritual journey that has since changed my life and my perceptions. From that day forward, I began making a conscious effort to have some "quiet time" to simply sit amid Nature's resplendence with a stone in my hand, listening. I ask a very simple question, then listen.

If you've read the *Conversations with God* series by Neale Donald Walsch, you may notice that his own walk with God began with similar circumstances.

What I learned that day, two decades ago, was incredibly simple, yet powerful:

I am worthy.

I also learned a different lesson. My idea was that, compared to God and all of Creation, I was too tiny and insignificant for God to bother with or notice. The problem was, I had things very backwards. God is much bigger than I imagined.

God doesn't care about financial status, or social status, or past "sins". It doesn't matter what type of home you have (or don't have), the car you drive, or the clothes you wear. Nor does it matter "what you do". You don't have to be some esteemed member of the clergy to hear from God. God doesn't care whether you're a CEO or a carpenter, a hired hand, a hot dog vender, or even a painter.

What matters is your heart.

The moment you seek him, He is there. Again:

When you can see God in small things, you'll see God in all things.

Never believe that God would refuse audience with any of His children, especially those who need Him most.

And this is the primary message of this book, for you to understand that *you, too, are worthy.*

I want to repeat that for emphasis:

You are worthy.

You are worthy of being inspired by God, having a relationship with God, and even openly communicating with God, because you are a part of God. You are a drop in God's ocean, a flake amid God's snowfall, a tree in the forest that is God. You are a part of the whole. A part of the body. And each part of the body is influenced by the rest. Which means….

Chapter 42 – Loving inspiration

It's not a question of whether a person's been inspired by God, the only question is: has that person realized it, or not?

At one time or another, we've *all* been inspired by God. Whether it's the striking beauty of flowers, a breath-taking vista of the vast ocean or distant mountains, or even through an act of random kindness, we've all been inspired by God, because this is what God does.

God inspires.

God is constantly changing and becoming a higher, grander version of Who He Is. And God accomplishes that through Us, by inspiring all of His creation to be a higher, grander version of themselves, God becomes a higher version of Himself. Just as we try to make our children the best they can be, God continually inspires His own children.

Whenever we act with Love, not Fear, we become a higher version of Who We Are. Whenever we act with generosity, not greed, we become a higher version of Who We Are. Whenever we give hope, not hopelessness, we become a higher version of Who We Are. Whenever we act with humility, not hostility, we become a higher version of Who We Are. And as we do this, with each act with Love and kindness, we inspire others to act more like God. Through one act at a time, we light the lights of others, and create a little more "Heaven on Earth". We give truth to the statement: "as above, so below". With our lights, we chase away darkness.

Chapter 43 – Practicing intuition

"If you follow your passion, it will lead you to fulfillment."

One of the easiest ways you can inspire others is by following your own passion. Whether it's music, art, sculpting, dance, acting in a play, writing, wood-working or hundreds of other activities, if you pursue it with passion to the conclusion, you'll find fulfillment. But don't do it simply for the sake of inspiring others, do it because it's Who You Are.

While it's important for us to be inspiring to others, it's equally important we are genuine to ourselves. I'm saying this, because I have something I want to share here. It would be easy for me to fill many pages below this one with various "how to" instructions of different methods of ways to connect with God (channeling, prayer, divination, etc.). But that's not Who I Am. Nor is it the goal of this book. I connect with God in my own way, and will share my own method, but I am not an authority in other means of connecting. They are simply not where my passion lies, and I'll leave instruction in those methods to those who passionately pursue those methods.

The method I use to connect with God mainly consists of intuition. I have experienced "automatic writing", even at times while writing this book, but automatic writing is not something I pursue. It is not my preferred way. It's something that happens to me in its own time. For me… for my path… I prefer a mix of meditation and intuition.

If you would like to try my method, below is a step-by-step guide. I would like to mention, after you begin a regular schedule of meditation, strange-yet-wonderful things will begin to occur in your life. In general, you'll feel more at ease with Life and a greater sense of contentment. You will also feel more as *a part* of Life instead of *apart* from Life. And in addition, you'll become more aware of the synchronicities that occur around you, and you'll notice "coincidences" that deter you from hardship and steer you toward happiness and fulfillment.

1. <u>Schedule a time and place.</u>

With life being as hectic as it can sometimes be (especially for parents), it's often hard for us to schedule a specific time to meditate. And if you live in the city, or have boisterous children, it can often be hard to find a place. For many of us, making time to meditate and commune with God is a luxury. I'd encourage you, however, to move it up the "priority list". Make it a priority… even if it's only once every week or two. Because just like working, or cleaning the house, or schooling, or whatever it is you do to improve life, connecting with God on a regular basis will not only improve your life, but can also improve your health.

And don't forget to quiet your cell phone. Sometimes just having a break from the phone is a respite in itself, and nothing can be more disruptive than a phone ringing during your meditation.

Also, set aside a place for your meditation. Whether it's at a local park, in the woods, or just stringing candles around the bathtub, create a space where you can meditate. And it's always a good idea to have a "back-up" location in case of inclement weather or other circumstances.

When I meditate, I prefer to do so aside running water. As mentioned, I'm very blessed to have 25 wooded acres, with a small stream flowing across the rear of the property, and a number of spots where I can sit alongside the small creek. In a few of these spots, the water trickles over stones or logs, and the quiet sound is very soothing.

On the other hand, never be afraid to substitute spots if you feel an internal urge to do so. On a few occasions, I've been headed through the woods toward the creek, only to hear a quiet "stop", or "sit here", and when this has occurred, the meditation was always very successful. In some cases, there was something I needed to see, that I would have missed, had I continued to a spot along the creek.

No church or synagogue pew can produce a higher awareness of God than sitting at the base of a tree and observing His creation.

2. Formulate a question in advance.

During that hustle and bustle that occurs between your meditations, write down any question you want to ask. And be careful of the wording. For example, if you receive a new job offer and you're unsure of whether you should accept it, don't ask "Should I take this job or stay with my present job?", because when you receive a "yes" or "no", which "yes" or "no" is it?

Instead, ask: "Should I take this new job?" Or ask: "Should I stay with my present job?"

Be specific.

And as a mention, I've found that when it comes to finances or material things, you sometimes won't receive an answer.

Whether you buy a new TV, or car, (etc.) or any other "material" thing is often "immaterial" to God.

3. Have a pen and paper available.

There are many times I've meditated without asking any questions. I've just opened myself to God to see what He would tell me. That's actually my most preferred method. And you can't imagine the number of times that the message I've received is incredibly profound, only to forget it an hour later. Or even during my walk through the woods back to my house. One moment it's in your head and the next, after a dozen deer buzz by, the thought is gone. So while you may remember the message, it's always a smart choice to jot it down.

4. Meditation … the act.

First, find someplace comfortable to sit or lie, and just rest for a moment, and relax.

When you prepare to meditate, your mind will often go into a stage of rebellion, hurling every worry and question and problem at you that it can. For this reason, I like to hold a stone to help "quiet the mind". What I do is just concentrate on breathing in, and as I exhale, I imagine all of life's worries and problems draining into the stone, where they are contained.

After your mind quiets, begin breathing in and imagine yourself surrounded by white light (or the essence of Life), and when you exhale, imagine the light (or Life) flowing down your body and out the soles of your feet.

After two or three breaths, ask your question, and continue breathing, just listening to what you hear.

If you get an answer (it may come later), or whenever you're comfortable stopping the meditation, stop and write down any message you received. Writing down your answer will mentally reinforce it and help you recall it later.

5. *Be* love.

Throughout this book, I've mentioned *being* love. That might seem a bit vague to some, so allow me to expound and help anyone who might not understand this.

Sometimes, instead of holding a stone, I simply think of my loved ones. I begin by thinking of the love I have for my wife, then my other "family" members (pets, who are masters at unconditional love), then my children, then grandchildren, then friends.

When you can feel all of the love you have for family and friends, begin turning that love *outward*, and using it to "love all Life you observe". Know that you have an infinite supply of Love inside you and you cannot "run out".

Love the tree behind you. Love the stream before you. Love the ferns on the hillside; love the squirrels in the trees. Become not just a recipient of Love, but a *source* of Love.

If you're not in the woods, in a bathtub or such, you can still find things to love. Love the candle. Love the fragrance it gives. Love the water and how it molds itself around you and feels. Focus your love outward, and mentally send it to your family and loved ones. See yourself as the veritable Source of Love, because the moment you see yourself as a source of Love, you are "being" Love. And as long as you can carry this feeling with you, you continue to *be* Love.

If it helps, imagine a brilliant white beam of Love coming down from the heavens (from God) and pouring Love into you. Let yourself become the "mirror" that redirects and disseminates that Love. You and God are One. You and God are in true "communion" through the "common union" of Love.

"He that loveth not knoweth not God; for God is love." -- 1st John 4:8, KJV

There is no higher action we can do during life than *being* Love, because God *is* Love, and when we choose to "be love", we are choosing to be "God-like".

"No man hath seen God at any time. If we love one another, God dwelleth in us, and his love is perfected in us. Hereby know we that we dwell in him, and he in us, because he hath given us of his Spirit." -- 1st John 4:12-13, KJV

If we always follow Love for every action and decision, we never harm nor abuse anyone or anything, because those actions are based in Fear and not Love. Just as darkness cannot overcome light, Fear cannot exist within Love.

"There is no fear in love; but perfect love casteth out fear: because fear hath **torment***. He that feareth is not* **made perfect** *in love"* – 1st John 4:18, KJV

In his book, *Be Love Now*, Ram Dass speaks of finding himself seated in front of a Hindu master, Maharaj-ji, and being immersed in an unconditional love that forever altered his life. He quotes the Maharaj-ji as saying:

"Meditate the way Christ meditated... he lost himself in Love."[xlvii]

When you are being Love, you are connecting directly with God. So, connect with that fragment of God that resides in you, then hang on to it with everything you're made of... because that's exactly what you're made of.

Be Love.

6. Cleansing

After ending your meditation, if you used a stone, take it to a stream (if possible), thank it, wash away "the worries" it holds, then let them flow away. Finally, replace the stone to its home.

If you use your bathtub, keep a bowl of small pebbles nearby that you can use during your meditation, then wash the stone you used, and literally watch your worries flow down the drain and away.

7. Waiting for an answer:

If you don't get an answer while you meditate, don't *be* discouraged. Every meditation session is different. I've had several where I received multiple answers or insights, and others where I didn't receive an answer at all. It often works like memory. We've all had that time when we're having a conversation, and suddenly can't recall a person's (or location's, or item's) name, and the more we struggle to recall it, the more elusive it becomes. Sometimes we feel like it's right "on the tip of our tongue", but we can't recall it. We've all had that "it'll come to me" moment. And typically, when we relax our mind by engaging in mundane, day-to-day tasks (driving, doing dishes, etc.), the answer pops into our head. Again, it relates to going "out of your mind".

For me, intuition answers usually work this way. It's rare that I receive an answer when meditating. I'll ask a question during meditation, will receive no answer, and then a few hours later, "poof!" there it is.

Some other thoughts:

For some people, connecting with God occurs without actually "contacting" God. I know that sounds strange, but rather than actually praying or meditating, they allow God to guide their lives by watching for significant coincidences, and following the indicated path of those coincidences. Anyone who has read James Redfield's *"The Celestine Prophecy"* will understand this. And if you haven't read it, I hope you'll consider doing so.

As another example, Carl Jung, the famous Swiss psychiatrist, wrote about "meaningful coincidences" and in his book: *Synchronicity: An Acausal Connecting Principle*. As a loose summary, he tied these "meaningful coincidences" together with other significant life events into the idea of a "synchronicity" which works within life and which we can follow.

A colleague and social media friend of mine, James Wawro, the author of *Ask Your Inner Voice,* describes intuition as "the awakening to the synchronicity of life". In his book, James opens by providing an insightful analogy:

"Getting intuitive glimpses into life's order is like seeing patches of light falling onto the forest floor. We know that a sun-filled sky exists above the forest canopy. We see patches of the reality of the sun, dappling through the trees. Similarly, through the seeming chaos of the material world, we begin to see spots of the undeniable coordination and harmony that exist." [xlviii]

You may notice that Mr. Wawro's analogy (of noticing light patches on the forest floor and linking them to the sky above) is very similar to the personal story I shared earlier (when noticing the sunny patches in the woods and equating them to the abundance of Love). This exemplifies the splendor magnificence of how God uses Nature to teach each of us. Two different people can each look at the exact same fragment of Nature and each learn different lessons. And there's a quiet beauty in that. The similarities in these two analogies also demonstrate the essence of synchronicity. We can each recognize a common thread that connects every part of the world around us, even though we may encounter these things at different times, and even in different ways. It's akin to putting together a picture puzzle. As we snap each puzzle piece in place, the larger picture begins to appear.

I'd like to add here that while reading Mr. Wawro's *Ask Your Inner Voice*, I experienced a number of synchronicities between his book, my own life, and this book. And when you experience these synchronicities, it instills faith. With that in mind, I'd highly recommend Mr. Wawro's book to anyone who wants to expand their understanding and use of intuition. In Mr. Wawro's friendly resource, he covers a number of exercises and ideas for developing and improving intuitive skills. He also provides methods of "testing" the validity of any message you receive and includes an abundance of intuition-related quotes from historical figures.

Other methods of connecting with God or Spirit:

For those who prefer, there are a variety of other ways you can open yourself to connecting to God or Spirit (your spirit guides, Guardian Angels, your Higher Self, etc.,) or Divine inspiration.

In her book, *Raising Our Vibrations for the New Age*, [xlix]author Sherri Cortland covers a wide range of these methods, including meditation and automatic writing. Sherri also covers using crystals, natural medicine, organic foods, and a number of other means to help in raising our spiritual awareness and vibrations. And while I haven't yet read her newest book, Sherri has recently released: *Spiritual Toolbox: Meditations and Spiritual Exercises to Expedite Spiritual Growth.*

One last thought:

Regardless of how you decide to connect with God (or Spirit), the more often you do it, the easier it becomes. As you become more attuned to Love and God, new channels of connection continually reveal themselves. It's akin to something I mentioned earlier. I've never actively pursued automatic writing. Yet often, while I'm writing, I find myself channeling a Higher Source.

After one particularly long day of writing while channeling bits and peices, I commented on Facebook that I was just over half-finished writing my book, and was really looking forward to reading it. To most people, this didn't make sense. After all, how could you write a book and not know the content? But to many of my Facebook friends, such as author Garnet Schulhauser (who wrote *Dancing on a Stamp*[l] in part while channeling questions to his spirit guide), the comment made perfect sense.

Working with your intuition and raising your spiritual awareness opens a multitude of new doors *("In my Father's house are many mansions..."* – John 14:2 KJV). But it goes beyond this. The more you practice, the easier you can slide into a meditative mindset. You reach a point where you no longer need to meditate to connect. Any time you relax your mind, it happens.

Consider this example I experienced:

One day, while driving a long, boring, desolate rural section of my commute to work, I happened to glance at a billboard sign as I buzzed by it. For the life of me, I couldn't tell you what the billboard said, or whom it was advertising. Yet one particular word in the text leaped out at me.

That word was "mindful".

I had no clue why it had stood out, but I sensed I should slow down and stay alert and be "mindful" of my driving. And mere seconds later, as if on cue, a herd of deer bounded out of the nearby woods and into the road directly in my path. Had I not slowed down and been "mindful" of my driving, there's no doubt I would have hit more than one of them.

Instead, I heard the message and was "mindful".

And....

Chapter 44 – Look into the Stillness

When you are mindful of your intuition, you gain a mind full of inspiration.

Just to clarify, the above "pearl of wisdom" popped into my mind a few hours after seeing the word "mindful" on the billboard, and then swerving to avoid a herd of frantically leaping deer.

This is how it works as you awaken to the synchronicity in Life. Often times, one single intuitive message can have multiple purposes. As you follow the messages of your intuition, you become aware of a beautiful synchronicity that's operating just below all the chaos and clamor of Life. And the more you listen, the more you hear.

Prayer is our voice; intuition is God's answer.

Let me provide another example. A friend of mine was once seeking a job. After a long morning of "hitting the streets" and going door-to-door submitting applications, he decided to break for lunch at one of the local fast food joints. Exactly as he reached the door, another gentleman also reached it, so he pulled open the door and held it so the gentleman could enter. The gentleman politely thanked him and they got in line and began chatting about the weather. After ordering, the stranger, who was dining alone, invited my friend to share his table.

My friend, who was ready for a little peace and quiet, was tempted to politely decline. Yet a little voice inside told him to accept the invitation. It was nothing more than a feeling, but my friend knew to pay attention to what seemed like "insignificant coincidences" because they often become "significant". As it turned out, the stranger owned a local accounting firm, and had a perfect job opening for my friend.

When you open a door for others, you sometimes open doors for yourself.

It was as if their meeting was "meant to be".

And this is how synchronicity works.

God resides in the stillness of life. God resides in the pause between cluttered thoughts, and silence between sentences, in the calm beneath chaos, and the peace within war. He is there in the whispers beneath Nature's clamor, and in the harmony beneath discord. We only need to *look into the stillness*, and suddenly He is there.

When you can see God in small things, you'll see God in all things.

To find God we must *look into the stillness* of Life.

Chapter 45 – Speaking for God

"It's good to want God to speak to you, but smarter to let God speak through you, because when God speaks through you, more than one can hear."

And this is where our journey together ends... at least for the moment. (Although I'm hoping our paths will cross again).

I'd like to thank you for taking the time from your busy life to read this book. I sincerely mean that.

Thank you.

My hope is that some of the messages contained within these pages – even just one of them – touches your life and allows you to makes changes for the better. I also hope that you find this book worthy of sharing, or recommending it to friends and loved ones – especially those who might need it most. Because through this process... through giving the gift of Hope, we bring light to the darkness, one candle at a time.

As one final thought, I'd like to encourage you to keep your relationship with God strong and growing. Doing so will truly enrich your life. And not only yours, but others. Because through that example, by letting God not just speak to you, but also *through* you, your light shines for others to behold.

Stave the darkness, friend. Be a bringer of the light.

Part 7:

An encore of miscellaneous "Pearls of Wisdom"

Contentment

The easiest way to combat greed is by recognizing the value of contentment and simplicity.

Oneness

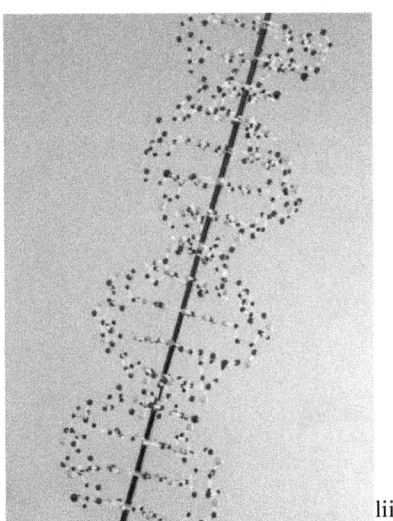
lii

*You can follow the religions where God is small,
or you can follow the religions where God is <u>all.</u>*

Faith

Whether or not you believe in God, He always believes in You!

God, Life and Love

God grew this.
Life grew this.
Love grew this.
God, Life, Love – Interchangeable terms.

Separateness

Nothing causes more people to deny God, misunderstand God, mistreat others, or abuse Nature more than the illusion of separateness.
Nothing.
No thing.

The Cold Shoulder

If you withhold love as a form of punishment, who is being punished?

Eternal Relationships

lvii

During Life, we cultivate relationships by spending days with others.
During eternity, we cultivate relationships by spending lifetimes with others.

Peace

"In war, the only true victory is peace."

About the Author

Donald Hicks grew up in the small town of Sardinia, Ohio. After graduating high school and a local vocational school, he attended Southern State Community College. He later went on to graduate Writer's Digest School. In the early 1980's, he and his wife, Arleta, along with their three children, moved to central Virginia. Since that time, Donald has authored five books, award-winning poetry, and numerous articles for a local newspaper.

Together with their pets, Don and his wife live on a small farm just west of Richmond, Virginia. Donald loves humor, and laughing at his own expense. He also loves being amid Nature and enjoys quiet walks in the woods, meditation, gardening, helping others, writing, reading, amateur metal detecting, and communing with God.

To contact the author, please visit his Facebook page at
https://www.facebook.com/DonaldLHicksAuthor, or write to him care of:

Nature's Path,
5721 Flinn Lane,
Amelia Court House, VA 23002

References:

[i] Woman meditating, royalty free image from Office.com (through Microsoft Word)
[ii] As quoted in *The authentic heart: an eightfold path to midlife love,* J. Amodeo, Wiley (2001) pg. 240
[iii] Girl and butterfly, royalty free image from Office.com (through Microsoft Word)
[iv] Girl and puppy, royalty free image from Office.com (through Microsoft Word)
[v] Hugging birds, royalty free image from Office.com (through Microsoft Word)
[vi] For One More Day, Mitch Albom, Hachette Books, reprint edition 2008
[vii] Success/Failure sign, royalty free image from Office.com (through Microsoft Word)
[viii] As stated by http://www.brainyquote.com/quotes/quotes/q/queenlatif587914.html
[ix] http://www.intouch.org/magazine/content.aspx?topic=The_Side_Effects_of_Fear_devotional#.VMQLSS50eJc
[x] Roller coaster, royalty free image from Office.com (through Microsoft Word)
[xi] Red curtain, royalty free image from Office.com (through Microsoft Word)
[xii] Martin Luther King, Jr., *A Testament of Hope: The Essential Writings and Speeches*, HarperOne reprint edition, 2003
[xiii] Autumn road, royalty free image from Office.com (through Microsoft Word)
[xiv] *The Hidden words of the Baha'u'llah*, 1985 U.S. Bahai Publishing Trust, page 52
[xv] Snowflake, royalty free image from Office.com (through Microsoft Word)
[xvi] Winding road sign, royalty free image from Office.com (through Microsoft Word)
[xvii] Calendar, royalty free image from Office.com (through Microsoft Word)
[xviii] Dictionary "Communication" image from Office.com (through Microsoft Word)
[xix] Boy and girl running in meadow, royalty free image from Office.com (through Microsoft Word)
[xx] Robert Fulghum, *All I really need to know I learned in kindergarten*, Ballantine Books, 2004
[xxi] http://en.wikipedia.org/wiki/Black_cat#cite_note-4
[xxii] Dinner table, royalty free image from Office.com (through Microsoft Word)
[xxiii] Watering flowers, royalty free image from Office.com (through Microsoft Word)
[xxiv] Couple serving in shelter, royalty free image from Ofice.com (through Microsoft Word)
[xxv] Dining family, royalty free image from Office.com (through Microsoft Word)
[xxvi] Candle, royalty free image from Office.com (through Microsoft Word)
[xxvii] Woman in church, royalty free image from Office.com (through Microsoft Word)
[xxviii] Butterflies, royalty free image from Office.com (through Microsoft Word)
[xxix] Children hugging, royalty free image from Office.com (through Microsoft Word)
[xxx] Girls gossiping about other girl, royalty free image from Office.com (through Microsoft Word)
[xxxi] Woman giving thumbs up, royalty free image from Office.com (through Microsoft Word)
[xxxii] Honesty dictionary, royalty free image from Office.com (through Microsoft Word)
[xxxiii] GPS, royalty free image from Office.com (through Microsoft Word)
[xxxiv] Girl chewing thumb, royalty free image from Office.com (through Microsoft Word)
[xxxv] Wooden path through woods, royalty free image from Office.com (through Microsoft Word)
[xxxvi] Green grapes, royalty free image from Office.com (through Microsoft Word)
[xxxvii] Plant in hands, royalty free image from Office.com (through Microsoft Word)
[xxxviii] Foxglove image, copyright Donald L. Hicks
[xxxix] Beech tree, copyright Donald L. Hicks
[xl] Three boys and dog, royalty free image from Office.com (through Microsoft Word)
[xli] Two girls and dog, royalty free image from Office.com (through Microsoft Word)
[xlii] Girl in road, royalty free image from Office.com (through Microsoft Word)
[xliii] Man meditating, royalty free image from Office.com (through Microsoft Word)
[xliv] Girl praying, royalty free image from Office.com (through Microsoft Word)
[xlv] Black-eyed Susans, copyright Donald L. Hicks
[xlvi] Writing music, royalty free image from Office.com (through Microsoft Word)

[xlvii] Ram Dass, Be Love Now, 2010, Harper One/Harper Collins paperback, pages 4 and 5
[xlviii] Ask your inner voice, James Wawro, 2010, Ozark Mountain Publishing
[xlix] Raising Our Vibrations for the New Age, Sherri Cortland, 2011, Ozark Mountain Publishing
[l] Dancing on a Stamp, Garnet Schulhauser, 2012, Ozark Mountain Publishing
[li] Girl in meadow, royalty free image from Office.com (through Microsoft Word)
[lii] Dna, royalty free image from Office.com (through Microsoft Word)
[liii] Man looking up, royalty free image from Office.com (through Microsoft Word)
[liv] Peach tree, Copyright Donald L. Hicks
[lv] Horses, royalty free image from Office.com (through Microsoft Word)
[lvi] Girl in therapy, royalty free image from Office.com (through Microsoft Word)
[lvii] Couple swinging, royalty free image from Office.com (through Microsoft Word)
[lviii] Cemetery, royalty free image from Office.com (through Microsoft Word)

www.ingramcontent.com/pod-product-compliance
Lightning Source LLC
Chambersburg PA
CBHW081013040426
42444CB00014B/3184